Basic Bible Truth

by
Aaron M. Wilson

MESSENGER PUBLISHING HOUSE
Joplin, MO 64802

Introduction

We are seeing in our day an outburst of so-called new theology and new doctrine only to become aware that the new twists are not so new, but a revision of the age-old deception which states "truth can be altered to satisfy one's own desire." I have felt the urgency for some time to return to the basic truth of God's Word, which will restore power to the Church. We now have a book to help accomplish this.

In this revised text by Aaron M. Wilson, we have a source of material which will be easily understood by a new convert, yet will provide a challenge to the seasoned student as well.

The author has written in such a way that the truth is dealt with in a very straightforward manner which you will find most enjoyable. Each subject is outlined in a concise manner for study purposes, which makes for easy reading. The author does not avoid any issues but has provided at the conclusion of each chapter a review with questions along with discussion on errors and alternative views.

To those of us familiar with Aaron Wilson, we know him to be an humble servant of the Lord who has again contributed to God's work, this time through the pages of this very special book. *Basic Bible Truth* will be a great blessing to all who read its pages.

James D. Gee,

Foreword
to the Revised Edition

Attempting to write a book which fairly represents the central Pentecostal position on the major areas of Bible doctrine is no small challenge. Although the thought of attempting this had been with me some years before the task was begun, I must confess that the responsibility to be honest, fair and complete was ever with me. To attempt a work in which such men as Myer Pearlman had written with such genius and lasting results was daunting. Yet, there seemed to be a need for speaking not only to the issues covered by such books but also to address subjects omitted from their writing.

I deeply appreciate the counsel and help of such men as Dr. Del Tarr and Dr. Ben Akers, noted scholars and educators. While acknowledging the help of these and other friends, the author assumes responsibility for the text with its shortcomings.

The original purpose for the book was to serve as a doctrinal text for the Pentecostal Church of God Minister's Study Series. Little did I dream when the work was being done that the book would receive such wide acceptance. It has been gratifying to see so many of the major Pentecostal bodies accept the book for marketing, and to see it become an entry-level text in colleges.

The textual revisions in this edition are primarily correction of such errors as have come to our attention and the clarifying of some commentary to avoid misunderstanding. The text has been completely set in a new and more readable style which should help the student follow the studies more effectively.

My interest in the subject of Theology and Bible Doctrine (in many ways, synonymous) derives primarily from my studies under such Bible teachers as Pentecostal pioneer, William Burton McCafferty. To such teachers and scholars, the Bible is a living book which offers the only reliable answers for troubled mankind. To love, study and know the Word of God is to build a reservoir of spiritual wisdom more valuable than any wealth this world offers. The early preachers and teachers of the Twentieth Century Pentecostal revival were people who loved the Bible, studied the Bible, and sought to live entirely by its precepts. I deeply appreciate that legacy.

In these days when the Pentecostal message has spread to countless millions around the world, attacks on the historical understandings which were founded on deep and Spirit-led study of God's Word, are common. It is vital that God's people have a firm foundation on the Bible and its truth, and that this truth ever be "rightly divided." It is our prayer that this book will help.

Index

1
GOD

CHAPTER OUTLINE

I. The Revelation
   A. Personal Encounters
   B. Covenant and Law
   C. Prophets
   D. Scriptures
   E. Jesus Christ

II. Proofs of God's Existence
   A. Creation
   B. Nature
   C. Miracles
   D. Prophecies
   E. Man's Need

III. The Nature of God
   A. God is a Spirit
   B. God is Loving
   C. God is Holy
   D. God is Faithful
   E. God is Unchanging

F. God is Righteous
G. God is Just
H. God is Merciful
I. God is Omnipotent
J. God is Omnipresent
K. God is Omniscient
L. God is Sovereign

IV. Names of God

A. Jehovah-Rapha
B. Jehovah-Nissi
C. Jehovah-Shalom
D. Jehovah-Mekaddishkem
E. Jehovah-Ra'ah
F. Jehovah-Tsidkenu
G. Jehovah-Jireh
H. Jehovah-Shammah
I. Jehovah-Sabbaoth
J. El-Elyon
K. El-Shaddai
L. El-Olam

V. Errors and Alternative Beliefs

A. Modernism
B. Spiritism
C. Christian Science
D. Eastern Mysticism
E. Mormonism

In that great faith chapter of the Bible, Hebrews 11, we learn that faith is the necessary requirement for approaching God. Faith is not the product of proofs nor evidences but rather proofs and evidences are the product of faith. Therefore we must approach the existence of God from what we call a "presupposition." The basic presupposition of Christian belief is that God exists and that He has chosen to reveal Himself to man. Notice that Hebrews speaks to this very thought: ". . . he that cometh to God must believe that he is and that he is a rewarder of them that diligently seek him" (Hebrews 11:6). The Bible never specifically attempts to prove the existence of God — it simply states that He exists. The simple opening declaration that "In the beginning God created the heaven and the earth" indicates that the existence of the Creator needs no proof to one who believes in Him. Although the Bible does not set forth proofs of God's existence as such, there are many proofs contained in the pages of God's Word which reveal His existence and His nature.

Once we assume that God exists and that He has chosen to reveal Himself to man the next question we face is that of how He has chosen to do so.

THE REVELATION

Adam and Eve walked with God in the Garden of Eden and needed no proofs or evidences of His existence. Cain and Abel understood the importance of worship, but only Abel understood the necessity of obedience. From the time of Adam until Noah men understood the existence of God and some walked close enough to God to have communion with Him. After the flood men walked away from God and although they understood the fact that God was to be worshipped they sought to reach Him through wrong methods. When God spoke to Abram and established a covenant with him, we find a new dimension developing in the relationship between God and man. Beyond the personal revelation which God gave to faithful men He now established a process whereby men might approach Him and be brought into reconciliation. The Covenant led to the Law including the many rituals which foreshadowed the coming plan of redemption. Consider the following steps in God's revelation of Himself to man:

1. Personal encounters
2. Covenant and Law
3. Prophets
4. Scriptures
5. Jesus Christ

This simple outline omits some forms of revelation such as that which we find in God's creation or through visions. It does however give us a simple straight-forward pattern by which God brought man from the devastating destruction wrought by sin in Eden to the plan of redemption through Christ Jesus.

I.   PERSONAL ENCOUNTERS

History is filled with records of those who met God in personal encounters. Adam and Eve talked with God after the fall into sin and God fashioned them garments and pronounced judgment on their sin. Adam's grandson Enos marked the time: "then began men to call upon the name of the Lord" (Genesis 4:26). Enoch "walked with God" and "was not; for God took him" (Genesis 5:24). Noah was Enoch's great-grandson and to him God revealed the coming deluge and subsequent preservation of creation. It was to Abram (later Abraham) that God gave the covenant and began a new process of bringing man into fellowship with his Creator. While the giving of the covenant and the resultant Law marked the beginning of a new level of divine revelation, God did not dis-continue His personal involvement with men of faith. The newer dimension only made it easier for men to communicate with their maker.

II. COVENANT AND LAW

God had made a covenant with man following Adam's transgression but this covenant did not contain specific codes of conduct. We do know that men offered burnt sacrifices from the days of Adam and that tithing was a practice of faithful men from the time of Abraham but there was no written code of ethics and behavior to guide men. With the establishment of God's covenant with Abraham we see a growing body of detailed laws to guide man in his relationship with God. The Law was made up of two divisions: the moral law such as the Ten Commandments and the civil law which guided the human relationships of the people of God. Man was given specific times and methods for worshipping and offering sacrifices. The plan of the Tabernacle was very specific and every feature and element foreshadowed the coming plan of redemption.

III. PROPHETS

When men fell short of obedience to the laws of God He sent special messengers to proclaim His words and to point men to God. Prophets also filled other roles at times, but what set these messengers apart as God's prophets was a divinely given message for God's people. The Law called for men to serve as priests and the priestly role was that of intermediary between God and man. The priests served by right of blood lines. Theirs was an hereditary position. The prophets on the other hand were men and women specifically chosen by God to give His message to the world. Some like Jonah were evangelists to people of other races. Others like Jeremiah were appointed to guide and comfort the suffering people of Israel. Yet, others such as Elijah were fiery voices of condemnation and judgment. All had specific roles to fill in God's communion with man.

IV. SCRIPTURES

Beginning with the writings of Moses God anointed writers to record the message which the Lord had given for His people. Some wrote history as a record of God's dealing with men. Some wrote poetry out of a heart filled with praise and worship for the Creator. Some wrote challenging words of correction and judgment as God burned His message into their hearts. All were inspired of God and all were used to bring man into a greater knowledge and understanding of his Creator.

13

V. JESUS CHRIST

Each method of revelation chosen by God has heightened our understanding of God's being and His divine nature, but no revelation is so complete and so perfect as that of Jesus Christ. When Philip asked that Jesus show him the Father, the Lord replied "Have I been so long time with you, and yet hast thou not known me, Philip? he that hath seen me hath seen the Father" (John 14:9). The Apostle Paul stated of Christ, "In him dwelleth all the fullness of the Godhead bodily" (Colossians 2:9).

PROOFS OF GOD'S EXISTENCE

Since the Bible was not written to prove the existence of God, do such proofs exist? Must God's very existence be taken by faith alone? Some people assert that intellectual honesty must deny the existence of a Supreme Being. Such claims imply that belief in God is some kind of an emotional crutch for the person who needs it. Marxist theories teach that religion is like a drug which appeals only to the intellectually inferior. Must we set aside our intellectual honesty to believe in God?

One of the most effective tools of secular humanism in our day is to belittle faith in God and insist that such faith is an emotional crutch. The very fact that the secularists present a broad and comprehensive body of speculation regarding evolutionary creation in the guise of scientific fact is itself blatant intellectual dishonesty. To read the decisions of courts regarding such teaching in public schools and to hear the blatant claims of the teachers and writers would make one believe that the theories are founded on a substantial body of proofs, or at least evidences which can be interpreted as proofs with some consistency. Such is not the fact.

The entire theory of evolutionary creation rests on severely faulted and inconsistent proofs. The fossil records do not support such claims but rather support the Bible record of the flood of Noah's day. Further, one of the most basic foundations of scientific teaching is that matter cannot materialize out of nothing nor change its volume. It may change character or density but it cannot grow from a void. Yet the theories of evolutionary creation claim that all which exists in the universe began without any intervention or action from a deity. No wonder the Apostle Paul spoke of the dangers of "science falsely so called" (1 Timothy 6:20). Consider these evidences which speak mightily to the honest seeker:

I.   CREATION

The scope and complexity of our universe staggers the imagination. The more man learns the greater is the wonder. Astronomy has continued to search for the limits of space only to find that our finest and most sophisticated instruments are unable to find those limits. The measurement of a "light year" is itself so large that our mind cannot comprehend it; and then the addition of numbers beyond our understanding multiplies those incredible light years so that the measurable distances in space become totally incomprehensible. Turning our instruments of research in the other direction we find that the basic building-blocks of nature are so tiny and so complex that even our

15

most powerful microscopes cannot discover the beginning point of matter. The atom is so tiny that only the most complex and sophisticated of microscopes can visualize it, yet the splitting of atoms can create explosions so massive that they threaten to destroy the world. The order found throughout all of nature is so consistent that it demands of our minds the admission that there must be a Supreme Being who brought all of this into existence out of nothing.

II. NATURE

It is amusing for the believer to read the suppositions of our day which tell us that over vast periods of time life began in water and then through a process of evolutionary change turned into ever more complex life forms. Even granted the billions of years they need to explain this theory, the very complexity of the system of reproduction whereby plants or animals can reproduce themselves with amazing accuracy denies such a theory. Not one evidence has ever been produced to show that one specie of creation has changed into another. If evolution could explain nature why are there no examples of this process of change? Certainly there are changes within a species amounting to differing colorations or sizes, but even the laws of genetics refutes evolutionary theory as an explanation for creation.

A study of nature not only impresses us with the complexity and perfection of creation but also with the wonder of its design. Earth is a "closed system" with every form of life important to other forms of life. All living matter finds everything needed to continue its existence. And man, God's highest form of creation, fulfills a very special role in the entire design. The perfection of order design and purpose cries out for belief in an intelligent Creator who created man in a wonderful and special way and for a wonderful and unique purpose.

III. MIRACLES

Not only do we see evidences of God's existence in the marvels of creation but He has visited man repeatedly and has wrought miracles in order to meet man's needs. In the Old Testament we find a wide assortment of miraculous events. Many of these miracles involved changes in the laws of nature whereby the sun stood still, fire fell from heaven and Pharaoh was astounded by the plagues. Others involved miraculous healings such as Naaman's leprosy and the raising of the dead by Elisha. In the New Testament we find a multitude of healings by Jesus and the believers who followed Him.

What is a miracle? It may be defined as the setting aside of the laws of nature. There is a natural process of healing built into the body, but such processes could never open the eyes of the blind as did Jesus. The very fact of such miracles with the resultant evidences demonstrates the existence of a God who cares and is involved in the affairs of men.

IV. PROPHECIES

Many of the ancient religions included forms of prophecy. The Greeks had their Oracles as did the Romans. Yet there is something different in the character and the perfection of the prophecies recorded in the Bible. Some of these are truly astounding in their detail and the perfection with which they were fulfilled such as that of Jezebel (1 Kings 21:19 and 1 Kings 22:38/2 Kings 9:36) and the altar (1 Kings 13:2 and 2 Kings 23:16). The imaginations of man might with shrewd guesses predict some things which will happen but consistent foretelling of events can only be produced through divine help. When we consider the large body of prophecies which foretold the coming of Jesus, His suffering, death and resurrection together with the perfect and detailed fulfillment of these, it furnishes a new level of proof regarding God and His involvement in the affairs of men.

V. MAN'S NEED

Genesis states that God created man in His own image. Involved in that act of creation is the inborn need for worship and the recognition of God. Studies have proven that every race of men, no matter how remote or how untouched by other races, has some form of worship and recognition of God. Those who have lived apart from God's revelation of Himself have entered into great error but the need for worship is there. It has been said that every man is born with an empty place in his heart in the shape of God. Until God fills that vacuum there can never be true peace. Even the most blatant atheists have fought with their unbelief when faced with the ultimate reality of death. Man's hunger for God implies the divine source of that longing.

THE NATURE OF GOD

As we study the Bible to see just what God has revealed of Himself, we learn much of His nature or essence. There is no definitive outline of this subject but the following will guide us through the Word of God to discover the outstanding revelations which God gives of Himself.

A. GOD IS A SPIRIT.

This is what Jesus taught the woman at the well of Samaria (John 4:24). In the light of man's long tendency to attempt the creation of some form of image or body for the divinity, it is vital that we understand that God cannot be localized into any form no matter how large or splendid.

B. GOD IS LOVING.

John the beloved tells us this in his first letter (1 John 4:8). Love is the very essence and nature of God. It underlies and controls all of His actions, even those which appear to be brutal or harsh. We are taught that we cannot bear the image of God in our lives unless we are loving toward others. No attribute is more descriptive of God's character than that of love.

C. GOD IS HOLY.

The seraphim in the vision of Isaiah cried out the holiness of God (Isaiah 6:3). Holiness denotes purity—purity of motive and purity of action. His holiness demands holiness in those who would serve Him (1 Peter 1:15 16). God can do no wrong because holiness and purity are His very essence.

D. GOD IS FAITHFUL.

"Great is thy faithfulness" cried Jeremiah even as he wept bitter tears over the judgments of God (Lamentations 3:23). The psalmist took note of God's faithfulness (Psalm 89).

E. GOD IS UNCHANGING.

In a world where change is normal and few things remain as they are for any great periods of time, God is unchanging. "I am the Lord I change not" (Malachi 3:6). It is the unchanging nature of God which made Him seem as an eternal rock to David and all who have found the security of trusting in a God who is unchanging (immutable).

F. GOD IS RIGHTEOUS.

The psalmist noted that the judgments of God are true and righteous altogether (Psalm 19:9). Righteousness might be defined as "rightness or the capacity and ability to be right at all times." Some have concluded that if God makes the rules of life, He can change the rules and play the game in which He is always right, but not always consistent. Such is the human view.

Although critics have pretended to see a difference between the revelation of God in the Old Testament and in the New, the fact remains that the God who never changes is also never wrong. His nature is consistent. He is not bounded by mortal weakness as were the fictional gods of Greece and Rome. He is altogether righteous.

G. GOD IS JUST.

The philosophical question of good and evil which asks: "If God is good and God is loving then why do bad things happen to good people" overlooks some points of Bible teaching. To evaluate

God and His actions from our limited human perspective is arrogance of a high order. God sees the whole fabric of life, and actions which may seem evil to us today may well prove to be helpful and beneficial when viewed through the perspective of time. The surgeon who cuts the cancer from a body will seem to be doing an evil and hurtful thing but his wisdom decrees that to leave the cancer in the body will result in a slow painful death. Justice is the product of rightness or holiness (see Deuteronomy 32:4).

H. GOD IS MERCIFUL.

In the fourth chapter of Revelation there is an awe-inspiring view of God's judgment throne. Here are all the aspects of holiness and justice, but the remarkable feature of the scene is that there is a "rainbow round about the throne." The rainbow has long been God's special symbol of mercy. Psalm 108:4 states that God's mercy is great above the heavens. The Bible is filled with references to God's great mercy.

I. GOD IS OMNIPOTENT.

This word is one of the three special words used to denote the unlimited nature of God. Omnipotent means "all powerful." The only limits to God's power are the limits set by His righteousness and mercy. While God can do all things He will do nothing that is contrary to His righteousness. He will not lie—He will not deny man of his free will. He will not make people be good or evil. The limits are not of ability but of consistency. Mythologies are filled with stories of gods who suffer from a variety of weaknesses and limitations. There are no limitations to the eternal God. He is truly all powerful.

J. GOD IF OMNIPRESENT.

God is everywhere—He fills all His creation. When the woman at the well of Samaria asked Jesus whether God should properly be worshipped in the Temple of Jerusalem or the mount of Samaria, she was told that the day was soon coming when there would be no localized place of worship—no mountain with special significance or presence—no sacred site to become a source of misuse and abuse. The glory and presence of God fills the world and He will dwell in any heart opened to Him by way of Christ's love. When the Russian cosmonaut boasted that he saw no evidences of God in space, he reflected the spirit that fills so many hearts. When the heart is filled with self there is no place for God. Yet the fact that his atheistic eyes saw no glory did not mean that the glory was not there. He is everywhere (see Amos 9:2-4).

K. GOD IS OMNISCIENT.

This special word tells us that God knows everything. He is all knowing. In 2 Kings chapter 6 we see God's omniscience in evidence as He revealed to Elisha the secrets of Syria to preserve Israel. Not only does He hear all conversations and see all events, He also knows the very thoughts of our hearts. Nothing is hidden from Him. This truth which is such a terror to sinners is a glorious fact for the believer who knows that God's knowledge assures His care. The God who counts the hairs of our heads cares about every aspect of our lives.

L. GOD IS SOVEREIGN.

Much of the teaching related to faith and answered prayer overlooks this vital truth regarding the being and nature of God. Certainly God answers prayer. He does miracles in answer to faith but He never abdicates His divine throne. He never becomes a puppet in the hands of man. He never assumes the role of the legendary genies who appear out of a bottle to grant men's every wish. His answers to prayer are guided by His love, His justice and His knowledge. We have the right and duty to pray in faith and to believe God for answers to our prayers but we also have a duty as Christians to accept God's final decision as being right and best for us. After all the promises have been read and we have followed to the best of our ability the directions for prayer and faith we must accept that God is sovereign and that He loves us enough to do what is best for us even if it means the denial of our prayer.

NAMES OF GOD

One way in which God has revealed Himself to man is through the names which He uses to describe Himself. Today we choose names because we like the sound or because we want to use a name of a person we love and admire, but in ancient times names were given to describe the characteristics of the person. Thus Jacob, meaning deceiver, portrayed the character of the man and when that character was changed through dedication, his name was changed to Israel demonstrating his friendship with God.

The names God used for Himself were often compound names, each element showing some particular aspect of God's character. One group of these—the so-called "Jehovah" group—is most significant. Before we consider these names we should consider the fact that serious Bible scholars are turning toward the more correct pronunciation of the name Yahweh rather than the older and incorrect "Jehovah." Why the difference? In the Old Testament text the name is rendered without vowels (as was common in Hebrew) and formed what is called the "tetragrammaton" or four-letter name for God: JHVH. The Jehovah spelling was created in the sixteenth century by Galatinus and never represented Hebrew usage. In the Hebrew scriptures the name, which means essentially "the One who is" was always written as JHVH. It was similar in character to the name of God given to Moses, "I AM." Because the Jews felt it showed lack of respect to pronounce the holy name, they always read it as "Adonai" or Lord when reading the Scriptures. Some translations follow this tradition in translating the name. Because the Jehovah form is so deeply entrenched in our literature and history we will use that form here; but newer texts will often use the Yahweh form for the same names.

A. Jehovah-Rapha (Exodus 15:26).

"I am the Lord that healeth thee." This name was used by God when He gave the miracle at the waters of Marah and it describes God's power and will to heal His people.

B. Jehovah-Nissi (Exodus 17:8-15).

"The Lord . . . our Banner." This name was given on the occasion of Israel's victory over Amalek. The banner was displayed before the tribes to

identify then. The Lord is our banner showing that we are His people.

C. Jehovah-Shalom (Judges 6:24).

The word *"shalom"* (and "salem") means *"peace."* Here the Lord identifies Himself with our peace. Even today in Israel the greeting of "shalom" or "peace" is given. Gideon used this name for an altar to God after his victory over the Midianites.

D. Jehovah-Mekaddishkem (Exodus 31:13).

"I am the Lord that doth sanctify you." Because the Lord is holy He cannot condone or dwell with sin. To sanctify is to set apart for holy service—to purify. The holy God provides a way to holiness for His people.

E. Jehovah-Ra'ah (Psalm 23:1-4).

In the beloved 23rd Psalm the Lord is shown to be our Shepherd.

F. Jehovah-Tsidkenu (Jeremiah 23:6).

To the weeping prophet Jeremiah God gave His name as *"the Lord our righteousness."*

G. Jehovah-Jireh (Genesis 22:14).

The first of the "Jehovah" compound names ascribed to God, this was on the occasion of God's intervention in the proposed sacrifice of Isaac and means *"The Lord who provides."*

H. Jehovah-Shammah (Ezekiel 48:35).

"The Lord is there" is the name God gave to Ezekiel for the coming new Jerusalem. This denotes His abiding presence which is promised.

I. Jehovah-Sabbaoth (1 Samuel 1:3).

"The Lord of hosts" is a name first found in 1 Samuel 1:3 and almost 300 times after that. The idea expressed by the name—that of God as the "General" of Israel's army—is ancient and in the Psalms is given as "Jehovah-Elohim" with essentially the same meaning.

In addition to the "Jehovah" or "Yaweh" compound names there are some built on the root of the "Elohim" name or "El." The name "Elohim" is very common in Scripture. Although this name is sometimes thought to be plural in form, this is not well supported by study nor is that assumption needed to support the Old Testament proofs of the Trinity as we will discover in a later chapter. The name "Elohim" signifies the fullness of God's power and might—the Creator God. Here are the "El" compound names:

J. El-Elyon (Genesis 14:18-20).
"The most high God" is the meaning of this compound name.

K. El-Shaddai (Exodus 6:3).
Also shown in Genesis 17:1 this name is translated as The God who is sufficient.

L. El-Olam (Genesis 21:33).
"The everlasting God." This name was ascribed by Abraham to show the eternity of God.

Another name used is "Adonai" meaning Lord. It is closely related to Jehovah and is used more than 300 times in the Bible. Unlike other names, this was not used exclusively for God, but when applied to Him was used to denote His supremacy over His people, and their acceptance of His rulership and authority.

Other names were used for God but these are the most common and are useful in understanding the nature of God and how He chose to define Himself to the limited minds of men.

V. Errors and Alternative Beliefs

Some errors and alternative beliefs are rooted in differing interpretations of Scripture. However the ones covered in this chapter are primarily the result of failure to believe in the accuracy and authority of the Word of God. It is not surprising that a man who denies the accuracy or authority of the Bible will be drawn to a teaching which denies his own responsibility to a Creator God and to the divine requirements for life. Here are some of the most prominent teachings which are at variance with Bible teaching.

A. Modernism.

Under this label we might include a variety of beliefs which are based on atheism or agnosticism. Two are Unitarianism and Secular Humanism.

Secular Humanism. Although the roots of such negative beliefs are found in ancient philosophies such doctrines have gained considerable hold on the mind of man in the last two centuries. They all share a belief that God is a fictional or mythical being created by man as an emotional crutch or to explain what his intellect can not understand. One popular phrase used by these modernists is the reversal of the Christian statement, Man is the noblest creation of God to say "God is the noblest creation of man."

While many of these give lip service to faith they teach that true intellectualism makes faith unnecessary. They speak freely of the "absence of proofs" as to the existence of God. They use ridicule and satire to avoid facing the unanswered questions regarding creation. From this denial of faith comes the evolutionary theory of creation. The absence of supporting proofs for their theories is seldom acknowledged. They teach their theories as if intelligence alone would support their stand. Some are fearful to flatly deny the existence of God, but doubt that He exists or can be discovered by the resources of man. (Some call such an agnostic a "cowardly atheist.")

B. Spiritism.

Called by its adherents "Spiritualism," this doctrine takes a variety of forms and is drawing many new followers in our day when men look for the supernatural without the resultant obligation to God. This is not a new doctrine, for even in the early days of the kingdom of Israel, God had to warn His people about the evils of such beliefs and practices. The use of seances and occult paraphernalia in our day is common. The spiritists will proclaim that they are "Christian" and try to give a show of orthodoxy to their practices. Leading liberal churchmen have been drawn into its errors. What does this religion teach about God? They deny the existence of a "personal God," teaching instead that God may be found in trees, heavenly bodies or any other form man may choose. We can get nearer to the true beliefs of this doctrine when we know that they speak of the devil as "our God our Father." No wonder Saul was warned to avoid the seances which were common in Israel in his day and met his death after conferring with the "witch" at Endor.

C. Christian Science.

It has been pointed out that this doctrine is neither Christian nor a science. Founded by Mary Baker Eddy and adhering firmly to her teachings, this cult teaches that God is "All-in-All and is essentially a principle." God is called the "Father-Mother" and the Trinity is denied except as fulfilled in the three principles of "Life, Truth and Love."

D. Eastern Mysticism.

Rosicrucianism has been an influential cult in past years advertising extensively and drawing converts. Today however we find a large number of cults based on the mystical doctrines of the East and all sharing a common foundation and many common beliefs. All of these deny the Christian idea of God and for the most part teach that God is a "high initiate or a highly evolved man. Most believe in reincarnation, and that God represents the highest level of such process.

One cult which has its roots in Eastern mysticism is Unity School of Christianity. They teach that God is "Mind, Idea and Manifestation." They glorify the mind of man and imply that herein rests the reality of God. They call God a "principle," an idea borrowed from Christian Science, while they hold to the Eastern mystical teaching of reincarnation.

E. Mormonism.

This cult appears on the surface to hold sound beliefs, but beyond their use of words, you find that they degrade the concept of God to teach that God is a man and that He had multiple wives, of whom Eve was a favorite; and that he inhabits space with a multitude of spirits, each of which is a son of God." They teach that God fathered the human race by uniting with Eve, a favorite wife. Thus according to their teaching, every man is a "God."

Why do men seek to deny the existence of God or to deny His power and authority? The answer lies in what faith in God implies. Because God is a fact of life and because He is as shown in the Bible men must give an accounting for how they live in accordance with the teachings of God's Word. The truth of God demonstrates the truth of judgment and the fact that we will give account for the deeds done in life. This is why so many people are seeking to find answers in the cults. They are looking for some salve for a guilty conscience—for some assurance that they can live as they wish without accountability. The truth of God's existence and character demonstrates the level of our responsibility to Him and His will.

Questions for Review

1. What is the basic "presupposition" related to God?
2. What was the purpose for God's giving us Law?
3. What role did the prophets fulfill in God's revelation of Himself?
4. How did Jesus reveal the nature and purpose of God?
5. What attribute of God defines his unlimited power?
6. What attribute describes God's perfect knowledge?
7. How do the compound names reveal God's nature?
8. What compound name describes the Lord's provision?
9. What name tells of his sufficiency?
10. What is the Mormon error related to God?

2

THE BIBLE

CHAPTER OUTLINE
Part 1: The Scriptures

I. WHAT IS THE BIBLE?
   A. God's Revelation of Himself
   B. God's Revelation of His Will
   C. God's Revelation of Man's Condition
   D. God's Answer to Man's Condition

II. HOW THE BIBLE CAME TO US
   A. Its Authorship
   B. Its Preservation
   C. Its Verification
   D. Its Organization

III. INSPIRATION
   A. Nature of Inspiration
      1. Theories of Inspiration
      2. Important Considerations
   B. What the Bible Claims for Itself
      1. Old Testament
      2. New Testament

C. Scope of Inspiration
1. Verbal
2. Plenary
D. Proofs of Inspiration
1. Internal
a. Unity of the Bible
b. Prophetic Fulfillment
c. Confirmations of Archaeology
2. Practical Proofs
a. Divine confirmation in prayer
b. Effects on mankind
c. Tests of Persecution

Part 2: The Bible and Tongues of Men

I. The process of Translation
A. Languages change
B. God's Purpose—Evangelism

II. History of Translation
A. Ancient translations
1. Greek
2. Latin
B. The English Bible

III. The Place of Modern Language Translations
A. The Need
B. The Problems
C. The Aprocyphal Books

Part 3: Errors and Alternative Beliefs

I. Mormonism
II. Liberal Theology

PART 1

THE SCRIPTURES

I. What is the Bible?

A. God's Revelation of Himself

The word which we use, "Bible," is from the Greek word *biblos*"(or *biblion* in some references) which originally denoted the papyrus reeds which were used in Egypt for recording writings. It was later used to mean "book." The Greeks used the word to denote sacred books and thus the term which we use to describe God's holy book. Of course, our Bible is more than just a book—it is "the book" of God and is in fact a collection of books or a library of sacred writings.

As we considered in the prior chapter, we approach God from the basic presupposition that God exists and that He has chosen to reveal Himself to mankind. The Bible is one of His most important tools of revelation. In the Word of God, we learn who God is, His nature and attributes, His eternal love for Man and His essential holiness. We learn of His supreme power, knowledge and presence. Without the divinely inspired writings of our Bible we would know God only through personal revelation or dependency on the revelations reported by others. Such, in fact, is the knowledge of God experienced by primitive tribes who have not been touched by the teachings of the Word of God. They live in superstition, fear and idolatry. Only by the Bible do we have the complete and authoritative revelation of God.

B. God's Revelation of His Will

Not only does the Bible furnish us with God's revelation of Himself, it also gives us a revelation of His divine will for our lives. Such statements as that furnished by the prophet Micah: "He hath shewed thee, O man, what is good; and what doth the Lord require of thee, but to do justly, and to love mercy, and to walk humbly with thy God?" (6:8) detail what God demands of His creation. In the early ages of mankind, in what we call the age or dispensation of conscience, there were no written scriptures. Each man knew God's will by conscience alone or in some instances, by direct revelation to the individual, as demonstrated by Abraham, Moses and other of the Bible leaders of that time. It was when man violated the will of God in Eden that the direct, continuing fellowship with God was lost. In time, God caused His revelations to be written so that these may be preserved and available to every sincere believer.

C. God's Revelation of Man's Condition

Along with God's revelation of Himself and His will, we also learn about man's sinful condition through the Bible. There are countless books of psychology and related studies which attempt to define the problems of mankind. Yet no scholar and no writings have been consistently accurate and penetrating with the exception of the Word of God. Different theorists have attempted to challenge the teachings of the Bible as related to man's sinful condition, but those teachings have consistently been abandoned as they were proven wrong, and the Bible has stood the test of experience. No man can know man's needs like the God who created man. The Creator alone has a perfect and unfailing explanation for the dilemma of man apart from God.

D. God's Answer to Man's Condition

Finally, the Bible also furnishes us God's answer to the problem of sin. It is usually easier to define a problem than to solve it. Even defining the problem of sin alone leaves man with the depressing realization that he cannot rise above sin and his sinful nature by himself. Therefore, God details in the Word the divine plan which was announced following man's fall into sin in Eden, and which culminated at the cross of Calvary. The Bible furnishes us a consistent and perfect pattern for deliverance from the guilt and shame of sin.

II. How the Bible Came to Us

A. Its Authorship

In his second epistle, the Apostle Peter reminds us, "For the prophecy came not in old time by the will of man: but holy men of God spake as they were moved by the Holy Ghost" (1:21). In what times and under what conditions did these "holy men" commit to written record the words which God spoke to their hearts through the Holy Ghost?

The Bible was written over a period of approximately 1,600 years and by approximately 40 different authors. The reason we have no exact dates and no exact count of authors is that some works are collective writings, and we do not always have a firm historical date to mark the occasion of the writings during some eras. Based on internal evidences, the book of Job is often assumed to have been composed, if not recorded, prior to the writings of Moses, but this is speculation. The earliest writings in the Bible which can be dated with reasonable precision are those of Moses—the five books which we call the "Pentateuch," or "five books." They are also referred to in the Bible as "the Law," even though a significant portion of the writings are historical in nature. The reason Job is assumed to have been composed prior to Moses is that there are no references to any of the Levitical forms of worship or to Jewish law anywhere in the book.

The writings can be divided into four major areas: History, Poetry, Prophecy and Teachings. Within these major divisions, you will find much overlapping, with books of poetry containing prophecy and books of prophecy containing teaching, etc. These only furnish us broad categories. In the New Testament, we use the term "Gospels" to refer to four books which tell the story of the life and teachings of Christ, and which are basically historical, with considerable teaching content. Likewise, the writings of Paul, Peter, John, James and Jude are referred to as "epistles," or letters, but they are basically teaching, and some contain a considerable body of prophecy and at times, bits of history.

The writers of the Old Testament recorded the sacred writings in the Hebrew language (with small portions of the the prophecies in Aramaic). The New Testament was written predominantly in Greek (Koine, the Greek language of everyday life), which was the language most commonly used for writings at that time. The Aramaic language was the language of the common people of the Holy Land in the time of Christ and was the language used by the

Lord. It was what the Hebrew language had become through the normal changes of language over a period of time. (It should be noted that some Evangelical scholars have recently contended with persuasive arguments that the New Testament was written in Hebrew.)

B. Its Preservation

How was the Bible preserved? Since Moses was educated in Egypt, and that land was the home of papyrus and the scrolls, we may reasonably assume that Moses wrote in this form. Many ancient writings were preserved in baked clay and indeed, entire libraries of these clay tablets have been discovered in recent years, dating from ancient days. However, the writers of the Old Testament appear to have used the papyrus or parchment scrolls for recording their inspired words. And since these would deteriorate with time and with use, they had to be copied to newer scrolls in order to be preserved. To safeguard the accuracy of this process, the scribes were men highly trained in transcription and they used a system whereby each letter was given a numeric equivalent, and the total of those numbers used to be certain that no errors were transmitted from copy to copy. No original manuscript of any Bible writings exists but we do have ancient copies, and tests with later copies, which represented several "generations" of transcription, reveal how accurate and trustworthy were the processes used by the biblical scribes who considered the quality of their work to be of great spiritual significance.

C. Its Verification

Since the writers of the books in our Bible were certainly not the only persons writing during the years of their life, what or who determines which are inspired of God? While some of the books do attest to the Lord's instructions to write some or all of the contents, others have no such recorded instructions. What is the measure and who applied it?

The Old Testament books were written over a considerable period of time and during the earlier years of Israel, the five books of Moses were given a special place as being particularly inspired, but other books were slowly admitted to the collection as their authenticity was proven or as, in the case of prophets, the prophecies bore the stamp of God's approval in their fulfillment. By the time the Jews were in Babylonian captivity the collection which we call our Old Testament was nearing completion and it is believed that Simon the Just, almost 300 years before the coming of Christ, placed the collection together essentially as it exists today and shortly thereafter the Greek translation—the Septuagint—was made in Alexandria, Egypt. This Greek translation was the one quoted by Christ and the apostles and even though the book arrangement and titles varies a bit from that used by Christianity, the contents are identical.

In the time of Christ, all believers accepted the Old Testament as the Word of God, and the only question raised was one of obedience—not of acceptance. However, as the books which make up our New Testament were in the process of being written, they were scattered among the believers and only portions were available as a rule in any particular location. Portions were circulated among the churches, but it was not until many years after the deaths of the writers that attempts to gather them into a common collection were made. The great impetus for this was the decree that Christians might be killed for possessing any of the "Christian scriptures." If the believers were to die for it, they wanted to be sure it was genuine. Both for this reason, and because there were so many false doctrines arising in some areas of the Church, the leadership began a program of collecting and verifying the New Testament.

Although the 27 books as we have them were in common use and acceptance for some time before, the final decision of acceptance was not made until the Council of Hippo, AD. 393. This was reaffirmed four years later, and the New Testament has since that time been the authoritative collection of inspired writings for the Christian Church.

The choice of the books was not made on some arbitrary basis, but was on the basis of recognition as being written by one of the Apostles or those who worked directly with them (such as Luke and Mark). It was also deemed vital that there be a complete agreement between the recorded teachings of Jesus and that in the writings. A word came into use, *canon*, which is a Greek work meaning "measure." To enter the canon of holy scriptures was to have met the measure of authenticity and divine inspiration.

D. Its Organization

Why is our Bible organized as it is? We should remember that the original manuscripts, with the exception of the poetry, were not divided into chapters and verses, but were continuous narrative. Those who placed the Old Testament into its present order arranged it by subject divisions and within those divisions, within chronological or date order. Thus, in the writings of history, you have the writings of Moses, followed by Joshua and then the writings of the Judges.

The poetry division begins with the oldest, the book of Job. The prophecies were divided into major prophets and minor prophets, not because of their relative importance, but rather because of their length. Within those divisions, the books were placed in the order in which they were thought to have been written. The same holds true for the New Testament, which is divided into the gospels, history, Pauline epistles, general epistles and prophecy. Letters to a common recipient were placed together, even though other letters would have been written between the dates of their own writing (such as Corinthians).

III. Inspiration

A. Nature of Inspiration

What do we mean by "inspiration" as related to the Bible? While the dictionary defines inspiration as "the act of breathing in," the meaning is narrower as we apply it to the Bible, for we might accurately define it here as "God-breathed." In 2 Peter 1:21 we find: "For the prophecy came not in old time by the will of man: but holy men of God spake as they were moved by the Holy Ghost." Thus when we speak of the inspiration of the Bible we are not using the word in the same way we might speak of Shakespeare or John Milton and their great written works. In fact, the Greek word which is our source for inspiration as used in 2 Timothy 3:16, "All scripture is given by inspiration of God" is composed of the two words *theos* or "God" and *pnein* or "to breathe." It is not enough, however, to understand that God inspired the Bible, for the very nature and scope of that inspiration is at the heart of our understanding of its authority. There are many ideas and opinions which have been advanced relative to this inspiration, and we include here some which do not represent the mainstream of Evangelical thinking in our day. Later we will consider the two terms which we will support here, "verbal" and "plenary."

1. Theories of Inspiration

As you might expect, there are an abundance of theories related to the subject of inspiration. We should understand the difference between inspiration and revelation. There are many revelations in the Bible in which God gives specific words to man, such as the Law given to Moses and the words of the prophets in which God told them to write specific words to people. However, there is a considerable body of history in which we see the recording of events. This is true for much of the writings of Moses and for writers in both the Old Testament and the New. In fact, we even find words of Satan recorded in the Bible. His words are not inspired, but the record made of them is divinely inspired. Thus, the Bible is inspired, but is not totally comprised of revelation.

Some see the Bible as being inspired by what is called "natural inspiration" or human inspiration of a high order. This would equate it with such authors as Shakespeare and Milton. Others teach that the inspiration of the Bible is "illumination" or spiritual insight and that it is similar to other books which portray spiritual insight. If this were true, men could still be writing scripture today.

Another approach is that of mechanical or "dictation" whereby men simply recorded words which God spoke. This ignores the human element in Scripture and would imply that there should be no difference in vocabulary or writing style between any of the books. A careful comparison of the contents would discredit this approach. Some feel that the Bible is inspired in part, and that the task of the Bible scholar is to determine what part is inspired. Another theory is that the Bible is inspired in thought or concept.

2. Some Important Considerations

Consider the problem if we might somehow convince ourselves that there is one tiny portion of the Bible which is not reliable — that is not inspired. Who will identify that portion? Who will define what is truly the Word of God? The alternative to faith in the Bible is to turn our faith to the intellect and mind of man. It is to make it a human book, a faulty guide to eternal truths. We cannot accept this position. We must not put man's intellect above the revealed will and Word of God.

B. What the Bible Claims for Itself

1. The Old Testament

The Old Testament abounds in the statement "and God said" or its equivalent. We find an abundance of instances where the prophets spoke as the voice of God and the words which they spoke were fulfilled in great detail. The Jewish people viewed the writings as inspired and developed a sophisticated method of copying to be certain that the words of God were not altered in any way. The New Testament confirms the inspiration of the Old Testament in a variety of ways. Jesus quoted from the Old Testament as the Word of God, and challenged the Pharisees when they ignored its precepts. The Apostle Peter told us that the words of "prophecy" came not by the will of man but as the Holy Ghost moved upon the writers (2 Peter 1:21). Jesus quoted extensively from the Old Testament as the Word of God. The Early Church used those Scriptures in their preaching and writing. But do they include the writings which were then being written as Scripture?

    2. The New Testament

Notice what the Apostle Peter said about the writings of Paul in 2 Peter 3:16. He quite directly referred to Paul's writings as "scriptures" or inspired writings. We have ample evidence that the Early Church considered the writings we now have in our New Testament as inspired, and as meeting the definition of St. Paul in 2 Timothy 3:16.

C. Scope of Inspiration

    1. Verbal

There are two approaches which might be described as verbal: the "dictation" theory in which the giving is mechanical and in which God may be said to have given the Bible "word-by-word" to the recipients, and the position accepted by most Evangelical scholars, in which God gave the content or message to faithful authors, but allowed them to express the message in their own unique way. A careful study of the Bible will reveal many differences of vocabulary, modes of expression and style. This does not mean, however, that these are written without inspiration or that they bear any less than God's total oversight and approval. While God did not make Joshua or David or Paul or John to become robots who wrote some form of mechanical transcription, He did give them His message, allowing them the choice of word patterns with which they were familiar. He gave total inspiration and approval to the finished writing. The "all" as used in 2 Timothy 3:16 is total and no attempt by some translators to make it less than total has succeeded. All of the Bible is inspired and approved by God, word for word.

2. Plenary

Another word, "plenary," defines the scope of this inspiration. It means "total" or "all-inclusive." This concept denies the theory of partial inspiration which would imply that only certain portions of the Bible are God-given or inspired. The Bible is totally different than other so-called "sacred" writings. It is God's message to man — God's only true revelation of Himself to mankind in written form. It is totally trustworthy, and is the only safe and reliable guide for time and eternity.

D. Proofs of Inspiration

1. Internal

a. Unity of the Bible

Why is it that so many avowed enemies of the Bible have studied it and changed their position to one of faith? One reason is the amazing unity of the Bible. Consider the fact that the Bible was written over a period of about 1600 years and was written by 40 or more men — yet there is no conflict in its message or its concept. The authors were men of widely varying backgrounds, ranging from shepherds to kings, and they represented a very broad range of backgrounds and training but their message is uniquely consistent. Even the so-called "conflicts" and "errors" which enemies have proclaimed disappear with careful study.

We can demonstrate the unity of the Bible by tracing out the themes which are at the heart of God's message. Consider the theme of redemption, which follows like a "crimson thread" from Genesis to Revelation. Other themes which are consistent are related to the coming of Christ and His glorious reign to come. The destiny of Israel is also a consistent theme threading through almost the total span of the writings of the Word.

b. Prophetic Fulfillment

Forecasting the future is risky business. Even with the most sophisticated satellite tracking and the known influences on the weather, our weather forecasters often miss the forecast. Modern-day would-be prophets and prophetesses such as Jean Dixon often base their prophecies on events which are reasonably certain according to historic patterns and past records, but they seldom have a success rate of as much as 40%. Yet in the Bible, we have hundreds of prophecies which were given and for which perfect and complete fulfillment came, often hundreds of years later. This record cannot be matched without divine influence.

The fulfillment of such highly-detailed prophecies with not one failure certainly attests to the divine origin of our Bible. Notable examples include 1 Kings 13:1-3 and 2 Kings 23:16-18; the remarkable prophecies of Daniel fulfilled in world history; and the large body of prophecies concerning Jesus which were so perfectly fulfilled in His life, death and resurrection.

c. Confirmations of Archaeology

It hasn't been many years since the critics were claiming that there were many cities and nations mentioned in the Bible for which there was no historical evidence. In recent years, there have been a large number of archaeological discoveries which have proven the existence of both. The finding of the Dead Sea Scrolls produced the most ancient manuscripts known and these proved the accuracy of the Scriptures as they have been handed down through numerous copyings by the scribes if Israel. The body of evidences supporting biblical accuracy is growing at an amazing rate and these are added to the large body of proofs supporting the divine origin of the Bible.

2. Practical Proofs

Not all proofs of the inspiration and accuracy of the Bible come from within its pages. We should understand some of the external proofs which powerfully support our faith in the Bible as the Word of God.

a. Divine confirmation of prayer

Prayer is an act of worship and religious faith. If the promises given in the Bible are of human origin, then there will be no consistency to any benefits to be derived from prayer. If our faith is founded on delusion and simplistic thinking, then prayer is a farce and our faith is in vain. What is the record? Not only do we find record of hundreds of prayers answered in the Bible, but history furnishes us with an additional large body of prayers which have been answered in miraculous fashion. There are millions of believing Christians in the world today. The testimonies as to great miracles of answered prayer are astounding. You may visit any of thousands of congregations of believers, and you will hear wonderful stories of how God has fulfilled His Word and answered prayers of every type. Such could not be if our faith were founded in promises of human origin. God proves the inspiration of the Bible by answering prayer and fulfilling His Word.

   b.   Effects on mankind

There are many religions in our world. Some of these are primitive and simple while others are complex. We might assume that a religion's merit may be confirmed by its effects on humanity. While there have been many atrocities done by professing believers, true Christianity has been responsible for producing many of the great humanitarian movements of history. These include medicine, art, music, drama and education. Some countries have tried to use Christianity to mask wrong actions. It has been the missionaries and the Church who have brought light and life to a world lost in darkness. When we consider the millions who have been delivered from alcoholism, crime and hurtful behavior, we can see a powerful proof of the Gospel's effectiveness, and of its genuineness.

   c. Its Survival

It is doubtful that any book in the entire history of mankind has been subjected to such vicious and persistent attempts to destroy it as has the Bible. Rome tried to destroy the holy books. Over and over, countries such as Russia have tried to obliterate the Bible from their society. Yet the Bible has endured despite every attack and has grown in circulation. The French humanist, Voltaire, proclaimed that in a hundred years the Bible would be a forgotten book. Within a hundred years of that statement, his house was serving as headquarters for a Bible distribution ministry and the Bible was read and loved more than ever before. It is Voltaire's own writings which have been forgotten. The Bible has been unique in its ability to survive every onslaught of men.

d. Test of Persecution

One test of the divine character of the Bible which is often overlooked is the fact that the early Christians gave their lives to possess its pages. Rome decreed the death penalty for anyone who had a copy of the "Christian scriptures" in their possession. Men will not die for human writing. Men will not die for words which are of uncertain origin. Yet those early believers repeatedly laid down their lives to hold to the pages which they knew to be God's Word.

Part 2

The Bible and the Tongues of Men

I. The Process of Translation

A. Languages Change

From the moment when the first words of Scripture were written, they were recorded in living language—language which changes over a period of time. The Latin language which is now a dead language was once the living tongue of Rome. The changes between classical Latin and its modern equivalent languages of Spanish, French, Italian and Portuguese have created almost totally different languages, with only similarities and borrowings of certain words and patterns. Similarly, the English language in which our own familiar Bibles are written has changed over the period of time in which translations have been made. The change is so evident that few people of today can read the early English translations, and even the original King James translation of 1611 is difficult to read, because of the many changes in spellings and word usages. Yet God has given us the Bible to be a living message and it must be translated in living languages—the languages of the people who are to read and understand its message.

B. God's Purpose—Evangelization

The Bible was given not only to teach those who have accepted Jesus Christ as Lord of their lives but also to reach those who have not made that commitment. It is a book filled with the message of God's love and His plan of redemption. It is God's purpose to reveal His will through words which may be readily understood. For this reason, Bible societies such as the American Bible Society have spent millions of dollars to furnish every major language group the Bible in their own tongue. Our missionaries depend heavily on foreign language translations of the Bible in order to share the message of the Gospel with other cultures. Yet there are many people in the English-speaking lands who have difficulty reading and understanding the older translations. For this reason, there is place for modern language translations in English, but there are also some very real problems which have accompanied the process of translation. We will consider these here.

II. History of Translation

A. Ancient Translations

1. Greek

As stated earlier, the books which comprise our Old Testament were written in the ancient Hebrew language and with the cultural changes which took place through the captivity of the Jews and the later rebuilding of the Temple, few of the Jewish people could read or understand the words of their Bible. Because the Greek language had become the language of art and culture during the existence of the Greek Empire, this use of Greek as the language of learning continued for many years under Rome. A group of Jewish scholars (according to tradition, 70 in number) in Alexandria, Egypt, translated the books which comprise our Old Testament into the Greek tongue. This translation was called the Septuagint. It was to be the Bible commonly used by all Jewish people, and became the basis of our own Christian Old Testament. It was also the source for the early translators of the Old Testament. It was only later that scholars returned to the original Hebrew as source for new translations.

1. Latin

As the Greek language slowly lost its place of prominence as the international tongue of scholarship, there existed a need for the Bible to be in the language which had followed the Greek, the language of Rome, Latin. Therefore, Jerome (340-420 A.D.) translated the Bible into Latin and this edition is called the Vulgate, or Bible in the language of the people.

B. The English Bible

Between the Vulgate and the ending of the Middle Ages there was little effort at Bible translation. In fact, people were discouraged from giving the common people access to the Bible for fear that they would turn away from the authority of the dominant church and the many traditions which had become so much a part of the faith. The first significant effort at bringing the emerging English-speaking peoples the Word of God was by John Wycliffe, who completed his translation of the New Testament about 1380. He did some work on the Old Testament before his death and his friends completed the translation.

For more than a century, there was no further effort at translation into English until William Tyndale completed his New Testament (1525) and the Pentateuch (1530). He was martyred for his efforts at reform. Because he was such a fine scholar, he had a substantial influence on the translations which would follow his.

A friend of Tyndale, Miles Coverdale, published his translation, based on Tyndale's, in 1535 and this was followed shortly by the Matthew's (1537), the Great Bible (1539), the Geneva Bible (1560) and the Bishop's Bible (1568). These followed the lead of Tyndale in refusing to base the translation on the Latin Vulgate alone, but utilized earlier Greek sources to give us credible translations.

The Roman Catholic Church brought out a Catholic version, the Douay, at about this same time and it contained notes which were not accepted by the Protestants, inasmuch as they attempted to give validity to the practices of the Roman church. Because there were so many translations with no common version, it was deemed essential to have one translation which could become the standard of the English Protestant churches. In 1611, this version, the Authorized (or King James) came into being. It was so successful that it soon replaced the earlier translations, and has had a profound influence on the English language. The King James version was updated for spelling and word usage periodically until the early 1800's; and from that time, no changes were offered until the New King James Version of 1982.

III. The Place of Modern Language Translations

A. The Need

In the centuries since the King James Version became the standard Protestant version of the Bible in English, our language has changed in many ways. While the King James Bible did have a strong influence in setting uniform standards for the language, no living language can exist long without significant change. Since 1611, the two words "thorough" and "through" have reversed meanings. "Let" did mean to restrain. "Charity" meant unselfish and pure love. While the serious student of the Bible soon learned to accept the differences between our spoken language and that of the Bible, people who had little or no Bible training were discouraged by the archaic language and unfamiliar word usages. To penetrate our society with the message of God's love and redeeming grace, Bibles were needed in words which were familiar to the man on the street. This is the impetus behind modern English translations.

Since 1880, we have seen the following translations come into being:

Revised Version (1881-1885)
American Standard Version (1900-1901)
Revised Standard Version (1952)
Berkeley Version (1959)
Amplified Bible (1965)
Jerusalem Bible (1966)
New English Bible (1970)
New American Standard Bible (1971)
Living Bible (1971)
Today's English Version (1976)
New International Version (1978)
New King James Version (1982)

New translations continue to appear. Each of these has found a following, but each has been rejected for various reasons by many scholars. The American Bible Society's *Good News For Modern Man* translation (TEV) was published to bring the Bible into what is called "newspaper English" for the man on the street, and it has been produced in vast numbers to bring the Bible into the hands of people who might otherwise never turn to its pages.

B. The Problems

New translations often meet with resistance from those who are not familiar with their approach or language. The King James Version was not received warmly by all scholars in its day. Yet the viewpoint or bias of the translators is vital to the evaluation of any translation. You often hear statements which imply that the new versions have appealed to older and what is supposed to be more accurate manuscripts than those available to the translators of the King James Version. The "older" sources used in most instances are the "Vaticanus" and the "Sinaiticus" manuscripts. These are considered by many conservative scholars to be manuscripts which were heavily edited by scholars who were influenced by doctrinal errors such as Gnosticism. These had been rejected by earlier translators as being corrupt and not true to the original text. In fact, the majority of the existing ancient documents are consistent with the "received text" as used by the King James Version. The influence of liberal theologians can be seen in most modern translations. The American Bible Society produced the *Good News for Modern Man* to reach the man on the street and it was at first a reasonably conservative translation, but later versions followed the liberal theology. The bias of the translators can be seen in such actions as the arbitrary use of "young woman" instead of "virgin" in Isaiah 7:14. Such influences are rejected by most conservative scholars.

Is there no place for the modern translations? Certainly, many Bible-believing Christians have found new understanding of the Word by the aid of the Amplified Bible, and have enjoyed the easy-to-understand wording of other translations.

The New International Version is a more conservative edition than most others and has been well received by many Evangelicals. Yet we must approach each with some care, for the Word of God is without error, but men are human and they can and do make mistakes. This is why the modern translations have had such a difficult time in replacing the trusted and loved King James Version.

C. The Apochryphal Books

In many family Bibles and some older editions of others, you find added books which are called the "Apocrypha." What are these? Are they the Word of God? The name, "Aprcrypha" means "hidden" or "secret" books. They have been rejected by most Protestants, inasmuch as they did not appear in the ancient Hebrew canon. They were not quoted by the Lord and were not included in the approved canon of Scriptures by the early Fathers of the Church.

Part 3
Errors and Alternative Beliefs

I. Mormonism

Mormonism is one of the chief proponents of the idea of an open canon, or continuing inspiration. They believe that the *Book of Mormon* and other Mormon writings are inspired equally with the Bible. In fact, they claim that the *Book of Mormon* corrects certain errors in the Bible. In their services, they quote the *Book of Mormon* alongside the Bible, giving it the same place of respect. It is from the *Book of Mormon*, along with the *Pearl of Great Price* and *Doctrine and Covenants* that they get their teachings which are so much at variance with Christianity.

II. Liberal Theology

Within the last two centuries, we have seen a systematic and powerful attack against the Bible as the Word of God. The early attack came from German theologians who sought to study the

Bible by using literary analysis techniques. Through this, they felt that the Pentateuch was written over a period of many years by a variety of authors. They found portions where the name "Elohim" (God) was used, and others where "Jehovah" (Lord) was the name given. Using critical techniques, these were referred to as the "E" source and the "J." Later proponents of this "higher criticism" felt that they had found even more sources. From there, they moved to various selections from the Bible, and convinced themselves and others that it was a human and faulty book. This approach has had a pervasive influence on liberal theology and we find varying degrees of its influence throughout Christianity.

Some feel that the Bible is mostly accurate, but that it contains some errors. Others feel that it is good for moral teaching, but is not worthy of complete faith and trust. Within these limits, we find teachers ranging from the orthodox to the most liberal. Controversy rages in some of our denominations of today related to the inspiration of the Bible. Yet the great vitality and growth of Christianity today is among those who believe that the Bible is the inspired Word of God and that the promises it offers us will be honored by God. And the greater the level of faith the more effective is the message and the commitment to fulfilling our Lord's commission to go into all the world and preach His message.

Questions for Review

1. What is God's primary purpose in giving us the Bible?
2. Over approximately what span of years was the Bible written?
3. What do we mean by "inspiration" as related to the Bible?
4. What are three proofs of the Bible's reliability?
5. In what language was the Old Testament written?
6. Why is the Bible translated into other languages?
7. What was the purpose for creating the King James Version?
8. Why are modern versions so popular in our day?
9. What does "Apocrypha" mean?
10. What is Mormonism's primary error as related to the Bible?

3

MAN

Outline

I. Origins of Man
  A. Creation
    1. Purposes of Creation
    2. Method of Creation
    3. Results of Creation
      a. The Physical Man
      b. The Spiritual Man
  B. Relationship with God
    1. From God's View
    2. From Man's View
    3. The Fall of Man
      a. The Image Marred
      b. The Road Back to Eden

II. Nature of Man
  A. Results of Sin
    1. Spiritual Effects
    2. Physical Effects
  B. The War of Wills
    1. The Moral Dilemma
    2. The Divine Solution

C. Man's Search for God
1. The Divine Discontent

III. Man in Society
A. Early Relationships
1. Patriarchal Society
a. Priesthood of the Father
b. Role of the Mother
c. Family Relationships
B. Man in Community
1. Responsibility to Neighbors
2. Relationship to Rulers

IV. God's Plan for Man
A. The Eternal Plan
B. Man's Destiny
1. Living Witnesses
2. Kingdom Plan

V. Errors and Alternative Beliefs
A. Secular Humanism
B. Mormonism

I. Origins of Man

"What is man, that thou art mindful of him? and the son of man, that thou visitest him?" asked the Psalmist (Psalm 8:4). There have been many answers suggested for who man is and where he fits in the scheme of the universe. Our primary concern is not the opinions of philosophers but the sure knowledge of who and what man is from the revelation of God who created us. The question of David arose out of his contemplation of the majesty of God's creation. He continued by saying, "For thou has made him a little lower than the angels, and hast crowned him with glory and honour. Thou madest him to have dominion over the works of thy hands; thou hast put all things under his feet" (verses 5,6).

A. Creation

1. Purposes of Creation

When God had options beyond comprehension, why did He choose to make mankind? In the account of creation in the first two chapters of Genesis, we find that God spoke all the worlds into existence, including all forms of life except mankind. Then God formed man out of the dust which He had already created, He breathed into this human the breath of life, and man became a living soul. Man was created in a unique way and for a unique purpose.

2. Method of Creation

The Word of God teaches that God created man "in His own image." Since the Bible also teaches that God is a spirit and is not limited to human form, it is obvious that there is something more than the physical body of man involved in this statement. The act of creation involved personal involvement of the Creator in the act of creating man as an individual.

This demonstrates the love and personal care of God involved in the creative act. The intimations of the Holy Trinity in the act of creation— "Let US make man in OUR image"—implies that man follows the pattern of God in more than a physical image. The very fact that the Bible proclaims the three-fold nature of man as body, soul and spirit demonstrates that man is in the spiritual image of God.

3. Results of Creation

When God created man, He established a personal relationship with him.He walked with Adam and Eve in Eden. He gave man oversight of all forms of life. Man became a partner with God in managing the wonders of creation. After the deluge, God again placed the responsibility for establishing life on earth to man. Genesis 9:1-4 shows that man is a unique creature, with oversight responsibility for the entire earth. Since man was created with a will and the option of disobedience to God, the fellowship was always at risk to man's decisions. Yet there has never been one moment of time when God has left man without a road back to fellowship with God. Not even the fallen angels were privileged to hold such esteem before the Creator or to have the right to God's greatest Gift.

a. The Physical Man

"I am fearfully and wonderfully made" said the Psalmist (Psalm 139:14). All living life is complex beyond understanding, but no creature is so marvellous an example of God's creative gifts as is man. Science continually strives to unravel the secrets of the human body and its wonders are beyond their genius. Man is God's highest and most perfect creation.

b. The Spiritual Man

What sets man apart from all other creation is not the wonder of his physical being, but the fact that God gave man a part of His own eternity, and man, having been made a "living soul," has a soul and spirit different from any other creature. Our reasoning powers and will are unique in all creation. Man is a moral creature, with a conscience and the ability to make rational choices. Animals learn to respond to hunger, fear or affection, but they have no power of rational, moral decision. Only man is endowed with this ability. It marks the special place man holds in God's eternal plans.

While the Bible makes no consistent definition of the distinction between the soul and spirit of man, generally, the soul is used to mean life and spirit is used to represent that divine infusion God gave to man which sets him apart from all other creatures. The "heart" is used to define the feelings and emotions, the "mind" is a New Testament word speaking of the intellect and the conscience is the seat of discernment regarding right and wrong.

B. Relationship with God

    1. From God's View

The brief story of creation pulsates with the love of God for the man whom He had made. We can only surmise the emotions of God which caused Him to walk in the cool of the day with Adam and Eve. We assume that God found a glory in the creation of creatures who would worship Him out of love and not out of duty—who would choose to obey Him and walk with Him. There is only one time in all creation when angels had the choice to follow God or Lucifer. There is no other record of choice or opportunity for decision in relation to the angelic hosts. Yet man was placed in the position of temptation and possible disobedience from the very beginning. The greater risk to the man whom God loved heightened the value of his worship. It is the worship of choice and not of force which blesses our God and fulfills our purpose in creation.

2. From Man's View

Did man need God's fellowship any less than did God? The beauty of Eden was not in the flowers or scenery, but rather, in the wonderful nearness of God. Man needed God's presence, but once sin marred the image of the one made in God's likeness, that fellowship was broken and shame replaced the joy of fellowship with God.

3. The Fall of Man

a. The Image Marred

Included in the form of man was the holiness which is God's nature. There was no breach of conscience because man was in perfect fellowship with the Creator. When Adam and Eve consented to disobey God, they knew instinctively that they were no longer holy — no longer innocent — no longer worthy of walking with God. The eyes which had betrayed the Lord could not look on His holiness. The hands which had plucked the fruit of disobedience could not take the hand of the Creator. The heart that had believed the lie of Satan could no longer bask in the glory of the divine Presence. The purity was gone and the image marred by sin.

b. The Road Back to Eden

The account of the events following the fall of Adam and Eve are tragic in the extreme. They were banished from the holy presence of God. The fellowship was broken and guilt replaced innocence. They could only look back at a flaming sword and a barrier between them and God's presence. The curse touched their lives in every point. Labor, pain, sweat and tears were their portion. Yet God placed a promise in the hearts of his fallen creatures, and from that moment, the plan of a road back to Eden was begun. Through Jesus Christ, man can begin the journey back to Eden—back to purity and innocence—back to the joys of God's eternal presence and fellowship.

II. Nature of Man

A. Results of Sin
1. Spiritual Effects

"The soul that sinneth, it shall die" says the Word of God. Procreation began after the fall of man. Adam and Eve began to bear children and inherent in the process was the seed of sin. Man, apart from God, is totally incapable of living above sin. All have sinned. All have failed in obedience to God. Therefore, the marks of death abide in all mankind. We are guilty both by inheritance and by our own actions. Because of sin, man is unworthy of walking in fellowship with the Heavenly Father.

2. Physical Effects

When Adam and Even sinned, they found themselves in a world which was a reflection of the broken harmony of creation. Thistles and thorns now inhabited the ground. Animals became savage. Disease and suffering came into existence and man bore in his body the marks of sin. The plenty of Eden was replaced by a world in which hard labor alone could earn a living for mankind. Woman entered into a bodily process which brought great pain at childbirth and she was brought into subjection to her husband. Every time we toil for income, we pay the price of Adam's sin. Every pain, every fear, every discomfort and the very fact of death comes from that sin. The natural process of decay in the human body comes from that source. The harmony of all nature and the perfection of man's overlordship were shattered with that first sin and all life is a demonstration of the price of that disobedience.

B. The War of Wills

1. The Moral Dilemma

In Romans 7, Paul presents a powerful discourse on the dual nature of mankind. Within every human breast there rages a war. The higher nature of man earnestly longs to do what is right and to walk in obedience to God. Yet, the baser nature of man rebels against all authority and seeks the fulfillment of bodily appetites and self-will. The holiest man never rises completely above temptation to do wrong and the most vile person knows moments of longing for release from guilt and condemnation. The cry of the Apostle is the universal cry of mankind: "O wretched man that I am! who shall deliver me from the body of this death?" (Romans 7:24). The answer to that cry is not to be found in philosophy or in higher goals for life. Within himself, man has no hope for deliverance. He wants to do right but evil is present and evil desires wage a relentless war against his better self.

2. The Divine Solution

The answer to the problem of sin and guilt is not in man's will but in God's provision. As we will consider in detail in a later chapter, God loved man so greatly that He provided the answer to sin. Man's will cannot provide salvation, but "whosoever will" may take freely of the provision which God has furnished through Christ.

C. Man's Search for God
  1. The Divine Discontent

Man has tried to put his own intellect on the throne. To acknowledge the existence of God is to confirm man's accountability to Him. Yet for all the vast experiments aimed at removing any thought of God from the minds of men, all have failed dismally. Communistic philosophy has tried to raise a generation who felt no need for God and yet faith prevails and the attempt has failed. The spirit which God breathed into man cries out for fellowship with the Creator. Reason cannot replace faith. Denials will never remove the consciousness of God from the hearts of men. Whatever his intellectual accomplishments and whatever his motivation, man will always feel within his being a longing for justification before God. God made it so.

III. Man in Society

Not only does the Bible speak convincingly about man's relationship with God, but also it speaks powerfully about man's relationship with man. Many of the social problems which plague our world stem from man's refusal to follow the guidelines of the Bible regarding our relationships one with another.

A. Early Relationships
  1. Patriarchal Society

From the time of Adam, early society revolved around the family and the relationships within that family unit were vital to human happiness and success.

a. Role of the Father

The father was the "priest" or spiritual head of the household. He was expected to represent the family in spiritual matters, and it was usually to the father to whom God spoke in times when He chose to communicate with the specific family.

b. Role of the Mother

The role of the mother was very different in ancient times. Marriages were usually arranged for purposes of family relationships. One reason for this was to retain the religious heritage of the clan within the family. The mother was the teacher, furnishing moral guidance to the children. She was expected to be a loyal wife, but her role was not one of meek subservience to her husband as some would imply. In Proverbs 31 we find a picture of the ideal woman and she is industrious and wise in helping the husband provide for the family.

c. Family Relationships

As the father was the spiritual and temporal head of the household and the mother was the moral guide and a strong helper for her husband, the children were instructed to give honor to the parents. The Ten Commandments included this admonition to honor father and mother (Exodus 20:12) and gave a promise of long life for so doing. In fact, under the Law, a child could be executed for a breach of honor. The patriarchal system succeeded in building strong societies because the glue of respect and honor made it so effective.

B. Man in Community

1. Responsibility to Neighbors

When Cain killed Abel, he tried to avoid his responsibility for his brother. He could not do so. As family units grew into larger clans and the clans grew into nations, it was vital that men have a system of justice to guide their relationships and to deal with disputes. God gave the Judges to bring equity among fellow citizens. Later, kings assumed the role of civil judges. Solomon showed great wisdom in dealing with these human relationships and the more just the civil government, the happier and more prosperous were the citizens. The Word of God places great emphasis on justice between men. The Ten Commandments forbid theft and false testimony in civil matters. Both the Law and the Gospel teach that we should love our neighbors as ourselves (Leviticus 19:18, Mark 12:33). Cheating in any form was rigidly forbidden, whether by false weights or by misrepresentation.

2. Responsibility to Rulers

The Bible teaches good citizenship. It makes no judgment as to which is the best form of government, but teaches that God is responsible for raising up and putting down leaders (Romans 13). Men are urged to be subject to rulers and to pray for them. In every form of government, God found benevolent and just rulers, and despotic and evil ones. Babylon was a dictatorship, but God found it "gold" in quality. Similar governments have been evil and injurious to men. The same is true of others. It is the justice and equity of a government which makes it right before God and men are simply instructed to be good citizens, praying for leaders. When injustice has existed, Christians have altered it by the preaching of God's life-changing message. When men are changed, so are systems.

IV. God's Plan for Man

A. The Eternal Plan

There has been much speculation regarding where the human race is headed. Some dream of a society made perfect through human skill. Others see men heading toward some form of "doomsday," in which society as we know it will be destroyed by man's runaway technology. The Bible teaches neither. It teaches that man will continue in the spiritual conflict until that day when our age will end with the sounding of a trumpet of God. Only in the Millennial reign of Christ will the aspirations and hopes of all mankind be fulfilled.

B. Man's Destiny

1. Living Witnesses

During the severe persecutions of the Early Church, martyrdom was so glorified by the believers that some began to seek death. One church leader proclaimed that the Lord needed living saints, not dead martyrs. In the 17th chapter of John, our Lord taught that we are in the world but not of the world. God made man to reflect the image of the Creator to all His creation. Through Christ, the image which was marred can return to a measure of His holiness. We are living epistles, seen and read of men.

2. Kingdom Plan

Jesus taught of a kingdom of God on earth—not the nearing kingdom of Christ's coming reign on this earth—but a kingdom whereby our Lord reigns in the hearts of believers. In the prayer which the Lord gave us, we find the words: "thy kingdom come, thy will be done on earth as it is in heaven." Amid all the imperfections and problems

71

of our age, the Lord is calling us to live out His love before the world and to share the message of His eternal love for all mankind. We are His witnesses—His ambassadors. Ours is a high calling, and God's purpose is being fulfilled in our lives when we obey our Lord's call and lead others to Christ.

V. Errors and Alternative Beliefs

A. Secular Humanism

There has been a forceful and highly-organized effort in recent years to remove all traces of Christian belief and practice from our public life. Our schools have been secularized so that there are scant traces of the Christian heritage which produced our nation and our social progress. This has been led by a small band of people who are called the humanists and known by Christians as the "secular humanists." They adopted a manifesto which denies the existence of a deity and proclaims man as the center of all meaning in life. They have been joined by some militant atheists, and have had a great measure of success in attaining their goals of secularizing our society. They believe in evolutionary creation and are the reason that textbooks of today present this theory as a fact, disregarding the substantial body of evidences which contradict the theories.

To read the suggested history taught in our schools, one would believe that such bold statements must surely be undergirded by a reasonable body of scientific proofs. These do not exist. Not one premise of evolutionary creation is built on scientific evidences. In fact, the very idea of a universe coming into existence out of nothing violates all rules of scientific thought. It is little wonder that the Apostle Paul called such baseless theories "science falsely so called" (1 Timothy 6:20). One danger of the current reigning thought is what happens when man puts man at the center of the universe. Men are then in control of what is important, and of all value systems. This is why the ultimate goal of the secular humanists is to control population both through abortions and through killing anyone who is thought to be non-productive or not worth living. Secular humanism cheapens life and takes real dignity from man, for they believe human life to be of no more significance than any other form of life.

B. Mormonism

Mormonism is not so extreme in its error related to the origins and purposes of mankind, but they do present some beliefs which are at variance with the Word of God. They teach that Adam found himself in a position which impelled him to disobey God in one way in order to obey God in another. They hold Adam to have been immortal and teach that sin comes from the sin of Eve and not Adam. Women can be saved, they teach, only through marriage to a Mormon man. They confuse deity and manhood, so that all men are viewed as becoming gods in the hereafter.

Questions for Review

1. How did the creation of man differ from that of other creatures?
2. What elements of the creation story indicate the presence of the Godhead?
3. What were the physical results of man's sin?
4. What were the spiritual effects of man's sin?
5. Why does man's nature draw him toward God?
6. What in man's nature tempts him to sin?
7. Who was priest of the patriarchal home?
8. Why are we instructed to honor our national leaders?
9. What is the highest duty of the Christian?
10. Why do secular humanists reject the idea of a Creator?

4
SIN

Outline

I. Pattern of Sin
- A. Temptation
  - 1. Sensual Appeal
  - 2. Promise of Desirable Effects
- B. Deception
  - 1. Challenge to God
  - 2. Appeal to Man's Weakness
- C. Disobedience
  - 1. Sins of Commission
  - 2. Sins of Omission

II. Nature of Sin
- A. Offense Against God
- B. Offense Against Others
- C. Offense Against Oneself

III. Effects of Sin
- A. Pleasure
- B. Guilt
- C. Condemnation
- D. Death
  - 1. The Unforgivable Sin

I. Pattern of Sin

The story of the fall of man in Genesis 3 outlines a pattern of acts and attitudes which led to the disobedience. The pattern is instructive, for it has always been typical of how the enemy approaches mankind and how he succeeds so frequently.

A. Temptation
1. Sensual Approach

James writes, "But every man is tempted, when he is drawn away of his own lust, and enticed" (James 1:14). Temptation is a strong urge to fulfill a sensual desire in a wrong way.

77

That urge may come from bodily appetites, selfish longings or unwillingness to control emotions. To what senses did Satan appeal with Eve? Hunger appears to have been an element, but the strongest appeal was to her desire to be "like God," not in holiness but in knowledge. While Satan is the source of temptation, the responsibility for resisting temptation is placed squarely on the shoulders of man—we are drawn away of our own lust or desires. Comedians have popularized the phrase, "the devil made me do it," but the Bible teaches that our own desires cause us to fall. In fact, the Bible clearly teaches that we will never be tempted beyond our ability to overcome. "There hath no temptation taken you but such as is common to man: but God is faithful, who will not suffer you to be tempted above that ye are able; but will with the temptation also make a way to escape, that ye may be able to bear it" (1 Corinthians 10:13). Temptation is not sin—yielding is.

2. Promise of Desirable Effects

Temptation offers a promise of fulfilment. Eve saw in the fruit the promise of knowledge equal to that of God. She was drawn by the desire to fulfill her own ego—to enhance her own sense of importance. Is not this the same sin which had caused Satan's fall in the first place? (Isaiah 14: 12-15) Narcotics are blighting millions of lives because of the promise of pleasure. Every temptation to sin promises something to the tempted, but as was the experience of Adam and Eve, the promise is never fulfilled. The Bible makes an interesting comment on Moses' choice: "choosing rather to suffer affliction with the people of God, than to enjoy the pleasures of sin for a season" (Hebrews 11:25). The plea-

SIN

sures of disobedience have a limit—are for "a season"—and this is followed by the penalties of disobedience. Many a sinner has boasted of the pleasures he enjoys, not knowing the terrible results when the "season" of pleasure has passed and the penalty becomes a reality. All the joys of disobedience are counterfeit. They offer no lasting pleasure.

B. Deception
1. Challenge to God

Satan knows the Word of God, and misuses it to his advantage and the destruction of naive people. Satan misquoted God to Eve, making the words sound like the divine commands, and casting questions on God's reasons. He placed God in the light of having selfish purposes in the denial of the right to eat of the tree of knowledge. When Jesus was tempted, the devil used Bible verses out of context to test our Lord. The advantage that Jesus had was His knowledge of the Word. Hiding God's Word in our hearts will keep us from sinning against the Lord. Satan tries to convince people that God is keeping some real joy or pleasure from them. He likes to cast doubts on God's reasons for denying people certain selfish activities.

2. Appeal to Man's Weakness

Every person is different and we all have different weaknesses or faults. Therefore, every man is tempted in a different manner. Satan knows our weaknesses and works against those. Eve envied God and was tempted to emulate His divine knowlege. Judas loved money and was drawn by the gold. Ananias and Sapphira loved prominence and lied to the Holy Spirit in order to gain attention and prestige. If an army has good intelligence, it will always attack where the opponent is weakest. The mature Christian will learn the devil's methods and say with Paul, "we are not ignorant of his devices" (2 Corinthians 2:11).

Because Satan attacks us at our points of weakness and desire, the Word of God places the responsibility on the believer to build defenses at those points of attack. The Apostle Paul never became self-confident when it came to temptation. He states, "I keep under my body, and bring it into subjection: lest that by any means, when I have preached to others, I myself should be a castaway" (1 Corinthians 9:27). Modern psychology tends to place all blame for weakness or sin on external influences. People are portrayed as victims — as helpless products of their environment. The Word of God places the blame on each person. That is not a popular teaching but it is truth.

C. Disobedience

Every sin is, in effect, an act of disobedience to God. While such is obvious in cases like that of Adam and Eve or of Israel when they made the golden calf in direct rejection of God's commandments regarding such, there are temptations which parade in a different light. Lapses of self-control such as anger seldom appear to us as acts of disobedience. As we consider the Bible principles related to sin, we will understand more of why this is true.

1. Sins of Commission

Some of the most obvious sins against God are the sins whereby we do the things which God has forbidden. Of the Ten Commandments, nine fall into this category. They are the commandments not to do such things as serving other gods, making of idols and such acts against others as theft and adultery. Only the fifth, "Honour thy father and thy mother" is a command to do something. To do what is forbidden is an act of disobedience and while all sin is in the final analysis a sin against our own bodies and souls, we must also recognize the truth which the Prodigal Son learned: "I have sinned against heaven, and in thy sight" (Luke 15:21). To do what God has forbidden is a sin against God.

2. Sins of Omission

Less obvious to some are the sins of not doing what we should do. "To him that knoweth to do good, and doeth it not, to him it is sin" (James 4:17). Some of the most grievous sins of our day are the sins of omission. These are the sins of the sluggard — of the careless — of the ignorant and of the selfish. We might list a wide variety of commandments to do things which are ignored by far too many people. In fact, Jesus restated the decalogue in the form of loving God and our fellow man. In this form, many sins are the failure to love. Ignoring Christ's commission to evangelize our world is a sin of omission. The sins of omission are subtle and are a great danger to the believer. Jesus stressed the importance of doing the things which He had commanded, for it is only thus that we are truly His disciples. Sins of omission should be understood and avoided.

II. Nature of Sin

A. Offense Against God

When David was brought face-to-face with his guilt by Nathan the prophet, he cried out to God:

81

"Against thee, thee only, have I sinned, and done this evil in thy sight" (Psalm 51:4). Sin involves who is in control of a man's heart — who is on the throne. When we substitute our own wills for God's will, we remove Him from the throne and elevate ourselves to that position of authority and power. Thus, every sin is a sin against God and results in replacing Him with our own will. This is why Jesus cried out in the Garden of Gesthemene, "Not my will, but thine be done." He kept the Heavenly Father firmly on the throne of his heart and thus avoided sin.

B. Offense Against Others

When we consider how many of the Ten Commandments deal with our relationship with others, we see that sin is a violation of our responsibility to our neighbor. Cain cried out, "Am I my brother's keeper?" but God put the responsibility for his sin squarely on his own shoulders. Every pastor knows the dreadful moral and spiritual fallout caused by sensual pursuits. The wreckage of lives caused by our moral laxity, incest and child abuse, are dread-ful to behold. While the penalty of a man's sin is not passed to his children, the resultant hurt and damage most certainly can have terrible consequences for them. Jesus stressed that we must treat others as we would like to be treated — the beautiful "Golden Rule."

C. Offense Against Oneself

The humanistic approach to guilt and sin revolves around the idea that there is no such thing as sin. People are convinced that God is trying to cheat them out of pleasure and happiness. The popular view of Christianity is that the Church is planting guilt in hearts and depriving people of the right to enjoy sensual fulfillment. Why did God determine that certain acts are wrong and sinful? We must conclude that sin hurts man. We are the most obvious victims of our own sins. No matter how much it might hurt others or how much it might deprive God of His just respect and worship, the net result is to destroy our own happiness, our own security and our own future. David recognized that he had sinned against God. The Prodigal Son realized that he had sinned against his father—but both had sinned against themselves. The Prodigal's father had lost his son's fellowship, but the son is the one who suffered the indignities of the pig pen.

III. Effects of Sin

Sin is deceptive because it parades in the guise of pleasure. In the heart of man is the desire for self-satisfaction and a heightened sense of self-importance. Satan used this against Adam and Eve and sought to use it against Jesus Christ. Every appetite and every basic longing built into mankind is wholesome in its purpose, but when man misuses or abuses these desires, it becomes sin. The appetite for food is necessary and pure, but overeating becomes gluttony. As our Creator, God knows about our desires and knows what are the proper and beneficial avenues of satisfaction. The frantic search of so many people to gratify every desire and the creation of new and unwholesome ways of such gratification are behind the growing incidence of suicide and mental breakdown.

A. Pleasure

There is no denying that the temporary result of sin is often pleasure of a sort. The glutton truly enjoys the eating, although the results are short-term satisfaction and long-term guilt and bodily suffering. The results of sexual permissiveness appear pleasant in the beginning, but the resulting guilt and pain soon outweigh any pleasure derived from the sin. Narcotics and drugs, both legal (tobacco and alcohol) and illegal, offer a temporary sense of satisfaction, either physically or socially, but the pleasure is of short duration, and the resultant penalties are terrible, indeed.

B. Guilt

The pleasure which Adam and Eve gained in their disobedience was soon followed by a deep sense of guilt. Such is ever true for the sinner. Our society has sought to explain the deep psychological wounds with some truly ridiculous ideas. They have blamed the Puritan influence on our society. They have eagerly accepted the explanations of Freud and we are faced with millions who are in terrible distress with no answer to be found in their psychology and psychiatry. It is no surprise that psychiatrists have the highest incidence of suicide of any profession. The answer to guilt is not found in psychology textbooks. It is found in the Bible truth that the wages of sin are terrible, indeed, and sin will bring its penalties to the sinner.

C. Condemnation

Guilt is the inherent realization that we have violated God's will for our lives. Our conscience tells us that we have failed, and the sense of guilt will bring us under the consciousness of condemnation. The sinner who holds unforgiven sin in his heart is as condemned before the courts of Heaven as are the murderers who stand for sentence before earthly judges. And where the earthly courts are subject to error, the courts of Heaven are faultless and the judgment is perfect and inevitable. The guilty may by guile and clever ruses escape the justice of our criminal courts, but no sinner will stand uncondemned before God. The sense of that condemnation is the heavy weight which each sinner bears before his Maker.

D. Death

"The wages of sin is death" declares the Word of God. The words of the prophet ring, "The soul that sinneth, it shall die" (Ezekiel 18:20). There are no more terrible words penned. There is no indictment more fearsome. And yet, like the citizens of Sodom and Gomorrah, many people walk arrogantly in their sins, totally unconcerned for the judgment which is pronounced upon their sinfulness.

1. The Unforgivable Sin

There are some compelling and disturbing words in the teaching of our Lord. "Wherefore I say unto you, All manner of sin and blasphemy shall be forgiven unto men: but the blasphemy against the Holy Ghost shall not be forgiven unto men. And whosoever speaketh a word against the Son of man, it shall be forgiven him: but whosoever speaketh against the Holy Ghost, it shall not be forgiven him, neither in this world, neither in the world to come" (Matthew 12:31,31). This statement, recorded by all three of the synoptic Gospels, is further supported by 1 John 5:16, where John speaks of the "sin unto death," for which there is no forgiveness. Those who have taught and preached this one biblical limitation of God's grace have been accused of using fear to gain conversions. Yet all the body of teachings related to God's wonderful grace must be understood in the light of this clear warning.

The Holy Spirit is God's divine Agent for drawing men to Christ. He fulfills the following duties to accomplish this:

1. Washes, sanctifies and justifies us in Christ's blood (1 Corinthians 6:11)
2. Confirms our salvation (Romans 8:16)
3. Seals our salvation (Ephesians 1:13)
4. Leads us in obedience (Romans 8:14)
5. Purifies us (1 Peter 1:22)

In the light of these vital ministries of redemption on behalf of our Lord and Saviour, Jesus Christ, we can readily understand why to blaspheme or to deny the Holy Spirit when we have knowledge of His reality is to cut off the road to God's forgiveness for our souls. It is also a serious sin to grieve the Holy Spirit or to quench the holy fire of the Spirit.

2. The Ultimate Results

The wages of sin are crystal clear from the teachings of the Word of God. God can never abide where sin pollutes the very atmosphere. He is holy and in His presence is purity. The wages of sin are death — spiritual death now and eternal death in the future. However, the good news is that God has a gift of eternal life for all who accept Jesus Christ and His sacrificial work on Calvary.

E. Two Types of Penalty

We hear much about the eternal penalties of sin, but there is another side to the wages of sin which should be understood.

1. Eternal

When the Word teaches that the wages of sin are death, it speaks of that eternal death so graphically demonstrated by our Lord in the story of Lazarus and the rich man. That death is a living death — a death where the "worm" of man's eternal existence does not die. It is not a temporary period as taught by some cults such as the Jehovah's Witness and Seventh Day Adventists, but an eternal separation from God and eternal suffering in the flames of a literal hell. The gift of God, through Jesus Christ, enables a believer to escape these eternal penalties.

2. Temporal

Some people feel that they have the right to sin without worry, for the Bible promises that God will forgive our sins through Jesus Christ if we repent and ask forgiveness. "If any man sin, we have an advocate with the Father, Jesus Christ the righteous: and he is the propitiation for our sins" (1 John 2:1,2). However, this forgiveness removes the eternal penalty but we will pay in the flesh for the sins of the flesh. Jacob paid for many years for his sins of deception. God will forgive gluttony, but the body will pay the price. The alcoholic can find forgiveness for his sins, but in his body he will pay the penalty. The sins of immorality can be forgiven, but the wreckage to lives remains long after the eternal consequences have been settled. God's grace and His love should never be viewed as a license to sin. Sin will pay its wages in this life.

IV. Universality of Sin

A. All Have Sinned

1. Inherited Guilt

The third chapter of Romans furnishes two statements which clarify the fact that all men stand before God as sinners. "As it is written, There is none righteous, no, not one" (v. 10) and "For all have sinned, and come short of the glory of God" (v. 23). This is a difficult truth to accept for those who have trusted in their own personal goodness. For many, holiness is the absence of intentional disobedience. It is not having murdered, stolen or lied. Yet David recognized that his sin was evident from the moment of conception: "in sin did my mother conceive me" (Psalm 51:5). This is the inherited sin. It is the sin which stains the soul of man before he has any opportunity to sin by choice or by neglect. Even if it were possible for a man to live above sin in this world, the guilt of Adam would be his portion and he would be under the penalty of eternal death.

It should be pointed out that guilt before God is not imputed until a person reaches an age where accountability begins. The baby is innocent in God's sight until the child is old enough to know the difference between right and wrong. The Holy Spirit is faithful to bring a child into the knowledge of accountability for one's own actions.

2. Earned Guilt

The Bible clearly teaches that all have sinned and that no man can live above sin apart from Christ. In Romans 7, Paul illustrates the futility of attempting to live above sin in the natural realm. The most careful person will sin, particularly when we consider the demands which are made for doing things which we prefer not to do. To live honestly and uprightly is certainly admirable, but it will not justify us before God. We are sinners by inheritance from Adam and we are sinners by our own actions.

B. Sin and the Conscience

1. The Role of Conscience

There are some who believe that men might be saved by a good concience. Certainly the consience is an important part of God's dealing with man, but there is no Bible evidence that men might be saved by keeping a good conscience before God. In fact, Paul told Timothy about hypocrites who had "their conscience seared with a hot iron" (1 Timothy 4:2). The conscience is a tool of the Spirit to help nudge us toward holiness, but it is not a safe guide to our eternal salvation. There are multitudes who can sin with no apparent feelings of conscience. Our justification before God is not a matter of feelings, but of faith and fact.

2. Sin and the Great Commission

There have been a variety of theories regarding the guilt of heathen races who have never heard of Christ. Some would teach that these may be saved by their walking in a good conscience. Others teach that God's mercy would prevent any judgment falling on people who have never heard of Christ and His plan of salvation. If this is true, then the most brutal thing a believer could do would be to preach the gospel to people who have never heard, for this very message would condemn all who rejected it to eternal damnation. Yet the Lord clearly intended that we preach the gospel in all the world and to every creature. This, balanced against the very clear teachings of Jesus that He is the only door to salvation makes the task of preaching vitally important for fulfilling God's purposes. Any attempt to justify another approach because it makes God appear kinder and more benevolent is a clear denial of the Word of God. God cannot be measured by human attitudes or measures. His ways are past finding out. We may not always understand why God works in the way He does, but we must accept the clear teachings of the Bible and walk in obedience to those. The justice and mercy of God are for us to accept—not to challenge. It is our task to reach every soul with the good news of Christ's redeeming love.

V. A Definition of Sin

The following approach to defining what is sin has served well, and may be of benefit to the student. Since God has created us with three elements to our being — body, mind and soul — we might test for sin with the following considerations.

A. Does it Harm Me?

Does the action harm me physically, mentally or spiritually? If it does, then it is sin and should be avoided.

B. Does it Harm Others?

Likewise, if it harms others physically, mentally or spiritually, then it is a sin and should not be allowed in our lives.

VI. Errors and Alternative Beliefs

A. Modernism

Under the general heading of Modernism, we will deal with some of the teachings related to sin which stray from the truths of the Bible. There will be some aspects of these which are shared, but the special approaches of each will be discussed as a guide.

1. Psychological Approach

With the writings of Freud, the father of modern psychology, and the host of practitioners who have followed him, we have seen a new falacy in relationship to sin. According to these psychologists, there is no such thing as sin. Every wrong is the result of influences over which the sinner has no control. Therefore, the sinner should feel no guilt. These theories are prevalent in our society, and undergird all of modern psychiatry and virtually all counselling apart from Christianity. In fact, some of these theories have invaded the church as counsellors have been trained in these humanistic theories. Such theories may make the sinner feel better about himself and may give temporary freedom from feelings of guilt, but the problem of sin remains and the delusions wrought by such fallacious theories have brought great suffering in our day.

2. Humanistic Approach

With its roots firmly placed in modern psychology, Secular Humanism denies any personal guilt by people for their sins. The word is abhorrent to them. The humanists tend to place the blame for all guilt or conscience problems at the root of "society." These humanists believe that a perfect world is attainable, but they view religion as being the enemy of progress. The more militant humanists (often in close cooperation with active atheists) seek to remove all influence of Christianity from public life. This is why the Bible has been removed from so many areas of influence and why multitudes refuse to believe that there is such a thing as sin, or that feelings of guilt are justified.

3. Universalism

One popular doctrine which is prevalent in widely diverse areas of thought and influence is Universalism. According to this theory, all religions contain much which is good, but there is no absolute truth. And since there is no absolute truth, there can be no such thing as sin. All sin is viewed as a "human frailty" and thus is not deserving of feelings of guilt. The universalists also teach that social perfection is attainable in our world and should be the goal of government and religion. These view the idea of sin as unjustified and as being a part of our Puritan ethic. The "brotherhood of man" and "fatherhood of God" sounds friendly and tolerant, but it is totally contrary to the plain teachings of God's Word.

Questions for Review

1. What does sin promise to make it so enticing?
2. What does Satan use to entice us?
3. What are the two primary types of sin?
4. Why is every sin actually a sin against God?
5. What makes sin wrong?
6. Can a good conscience bring salvation?
7. Why is it so vital that we fulfill the Great Commission?
8. Is God unjust to condemn ignorant people to eternal death?
9. What is the role of the Holy Spirit in salvation?
10. What is the major fallacy of modernism as related to sin?

5

JESUS CHRIST

Outline

I. His Deity
  A. Pre-existence
    1. Old Testament Evidences
    2. New Testament Teachings
  B. His Identity with the Father
    1. What Jesus Claimed
    2. What Others Taught
      a. His Disciples
      b. Demon Testimony
  C. His Divine Nature
    1. His Teachings
    2. His Actions
    3. His Acceptance of Worship
    4. His Sinless Life
    5. His Forgiving of Sins
  D. God With Us — The Divine Bridge
    1. The Problem
    2. The Second Adam
II. His Humanity
  A. His Birth

1. Human Family
2. Human Characteristics
B. His Limitations
    1. God in Human Flesh
    2. His Purpose
C. Human Identity
    1. The Son of Man
    2. The Loving Physician

III. His Death and Resurrection
A. His Death
    1. Prophecies
    2. Fulfillment
B. His Resurrection
    1. The Necessity
    2. The Purpose
    3. The Implication

IV. His Offices
A. Prophet
    1. God to Man
    2. His Infallible Words
B. Priest
    1. Man to God
    2. Fulfillment of Calvary
C. King
    1. Man to Man
    2. Character of His Kingdom
D. Attorney
    1. The Concept
    2. The Purpose

V. Errors and Alternative Beliefs
A. Christian Science
B. Mormonism
C. Jehovah's Witnesses
D. Liberal Theology

I. His Deity

There is no truth so vital to Christianity as the person and work of Jesus Christ. In the Early Church, His life, work, death and resurrection were the crucial tests of orthodoxy for the believer. Our understanding of just who and what Jesus was and is can be supported by a very large volume of Scripture. We will only consider some of the typical texts which confirm what the Bible teaches about our Lord and Saviour, Jesus Christ, for these truths literally breathe from the pages of the Bible from beginning to end.

A. Pre-existence

1. Old Testament Evidences

What does the Old Testament teach us about the pre-existence of Jesus Christ? Here we must see the implications of a number of references which do not specifically name Jesus, but clearly imply His presence with the Father before His incarnation. In the story of creation, we find God the Father speaking to a partner in the creation, saying "let us make man in our image." Nowhere are there evidences that God would have included angels in such a task. Clearly, the Father was speaking to Jesus, who shared the task of creation with the Father. In Micah 5:2, we see that the Messiah who was to be born in Bethlehem had a pre-existence: ". . . out of thee shall come forth unto me that is to be ruler in Isael; whose goings forth have been from of old, from everlasting."

2. New Testament Teachings

In the opening chapter of his Gospel, John clearly teaches that Jesus was with God in the beginning and shared in the creation of all things.

In John 8, we see some powerful statements of Jesus related to his pre-incarnate existence. In verse 38, He speaks of the things He has "seen" with the Heavenly Father, and in verse 58, He states, "before Abraham was, I am." His use of the "I am" phrase clearly identifies Him with God the Father who sent the message to Pharaoh that "I AM" had sent him.

B. His Identity with the Father

1. What Jesus Claimed

While there are people who will state that Jesus never claimed to be the Son of God, the Bible clearly shows otherwise. In Matthew 11:27, Jesus says that all things were delivered to Him from the Father and no man could know the Father except Jesus make the revelation. In the 17th chapter of John, the Lord reveals His pre-existence (v. 5, ". . . the glory I had with thee before the world was") and states clearly His unique relationship to the Father. In John 3:16, Jesus said that He was the "only begotten son" of God, and the implication in the original tongue is that Jesus is the "uniquely begotten" Son. The Heavenly Father has other children and in fact, every believer is made an heir of God and a joint-heir with Jesus Christ, but no other "son" of God is son in the same way as our Lord. His relationship was and is unique. Therefore, He could honestly state that no other one could truly and fully reveal the Father but Himself, for He alone was in that special relationship.

2. What Others Taught

a. His Followers

The prophet Isaiah foretold that Jesus would be "The mighty God" (Isaiah 9:6), and this is confirmed by those who followed the Lord's ministry with the fulfilling of His commission. In Colossians 2:9, the Apostle Paul states, "For in him dwelleth all the fulness of the Godhead bodily." In 1 Corinthians 15:47, Jesus is called "the Lord from heaven." Again, in 1 Timothy 6:15, Jesus is called ". . . King of kings, and Lord of lords." He was consistently presented by the Early Church as divine—the Son of God and the coming King of glory.

 b. Demon Testimony

Some may not find it surprising that our Lord's followers always spoke of Him as divine, but who would expect confirmation of His deity to come from satanic sources? In Luke 4:41, we find just such confirmation, but the Lord refused to allow them to continue to speak, awaiting the time when the revelation would be in God's timing and not in the devil's.

C. His Divine Nature

 1. His Teachings

In the light of His many statements referring to Himself as the Son of Man, some have contended that Jesus never claimed to be divine. What did He teach regarding His own divinity? Clearly, Jesus taught that He was "in" the Father and the Father in Him. He said in John 8:23,24 ". . . I am not of this world. I said therefore unto you, that ye shall die in your sins: for if ye believe not that I am he, ye shall die in your sins." In this and in John 18:5, there is special meaning to the choice of words, "I am," for to the Jewish mind, Jesus was clearly claiming identity with Jehovah, the I AM of the Old Testament. This is why they sought to stone him in the first reference and fell back before Him in the second.

In His teachings, Jesus not only claimed special identity with God the Father, but the very nature of His teachings proclaimed His source of knowledge as higher than mortal. Over and over the people stated that no man had ever taught as did our Lord. He taught with authority born of His pre-existence in the courts of Heaven. His teachings bore the stamp of divine source and authority, and history has proven the accuracy of His statements and claims. His prophecies have been fulfilled. His promises have been honored.

2. His Actions

If "actions speak louder than words," what do the actions of Jesus tell us about His divinity? Jesus was not the first to work miracles, for many of the prophets before Him had also done mighty works by the power of God. Yet the miracles of Jesus bore a remarkable difference, in that He spoke with divine authority and things happened. Storms were stilled on the sea. Demons departed, after addressing Him as the Son of God. Elijah was miraculously fed, but Jesus miraculously fed multitudes. His actions bear testimony to His divinity.

3. His Acceptance of Worship

Not one statement of our Lord demonstrated any willingness to violate a single precept of Bible teachings. He told the rich young ruler to keep the commandments. Jesus criticized the Pharisees for violating these same commandments by their devious rulings or traditions. Yet Jesus accepted worship of a leper (Matthew 8:2), a ruler (Matthew 9:18), and the disciples following the stilling of the storm (Matthew 14:33). They called Him "God" and He made no challenge. After His resurrection,

BASIC BIBLE TRUTH

Thomas called Him Lord and God (John 20:28). To accept worship without being divine was to make one of the most serious infractions of the Law possible to man. Yet, our Lord accepted praise and worship as His due. At the triumphant entry, some Pharisees tried to stop the adulation. Jesus answered, "I tell you that, if these should hold their peace, the stones would immediately cry out" (Luke 19:40).

4. His Sinless Life

The Bible teaches that all men have sinned and come short of the glory of God. The only record in existence of one who lived above sin was our Lord. His birth was unique in that He was born of a virgin, having been fathered by the Holy Ghost (Matthew 1:18; Luke 1:35). In the eighth chapter of John, there are some remarkable statements of Jesus related to sin. He asked the scribes and Pharisees who were without sin to cast stones at the woman brought to Him for conviction. None could do so. He challenged them to accuse Him of sin, but none could do it. "Ye are from beneath; I am from above" He states (v. 23). 2 Corinthians 5:21 and Hebrews 4:15 confirm that Jesus lived without sin. No man could live such a sinless life—only our Lord.

5. His Forgiving of Sins

The scribes of Capernaum challenged Jesus when He forgave the sins of the palsied man (Mark 2:5-10). When Jesus was guest at a Pharisee's home, a woman who was known as a great sinner came to the Lord (Luke 7:36-50). Jesus forgave her sins and demonstrated His right to do so. To the thief on the cross, He gave the promise that the repentent man would that day be with Jesus in Paradise.

D. God With Us—The Divine Bridge

1. The Problem

When Adam and Eve walked in innocence in the Garden of Eden, there was no problem of communication between God and man. Man could freely fellowship with His Creator. When man fell into sin through disobedience, that bond of communication was broken. God could not look on sin and could not fellowship with man. Therefore, man was banished from the Garden of Eden and sentenced to suffer the penalties for his sin. Man's very nature was changed by that sinful act and since that time, all men have borne the results of that Adamic nature in their bodies. To the serpent, God said: "I will put enmity between thee and the woman, and between thy seed and her seed; and it shall bruise thy head, and thou shalt bruise his heel" (Genesis 3:15).

God killed animals to make a covering for Adam and Eve, offering the first blood sacrifice. A plan was begun which would point to a day when God would perfect a plan for restoring men to fellowship with Himself. For this, God would need an intermediary who could fulfill all aspects of God's divine plan and bring man back into fellowship with God. Therefore, the angel proclaimed that the name of the Babe born in the manger would be ". . . Emanuel, which being interpreted is, God with us" (Matthew 1:23).

2. The Second Adam

When the first Adam failed the test of temptation and sinned, he brought all men under the penalty of death. The Heavenly Father needed a "second Adam" to go through temptation, yet without sin. This is the role which Christ fulfilled. In Romans 5, Paul discusses the appropriate way in which God reversed the sentence of Adam through the "second Adam," Christ. In Him, God perfected the bridge of communication between a holy God and sinful man.

II. His Humanity

One of the most difficult of Bible truths to explain rationally is the apparent conflict between Christ's divinity and His humanity. The Early Church addressed this issue and resolved it by stating simply that God was truly God and truly man. Attempts to rationalize this apparent conflict have introduced errors both by those who stressed His humanity to the point that they denied His deity and those who stressed His deity to the exclusion of His humanity. We will learn that the Bible teaches both, and does not fully explain what appears to man to be a conflict. He was truly God and truly man.

A. His Birth
1. Human Family
The birth of Jesus Christ was unique in that He was born of a mortal mother, but conceived by the Holy Ghost rather than a human father. While there are some brief glimpses of His consciousness of divinity during His childhood, such as the events in the Temple following His "bar mitzvah" (Luke 2:41-49), it appears that our Lord grew up much as other children of His day did. He was subject to His parents and evidently shared in the duties of the carpenter shop with Joseph. It ap-

pears that Joseph had died by the time Jesus came into mature years and began His earthly ministry, for there is mention only of His mother at that time and following.

2. Human Characteristics

Jesus lived much as did other members of His own earthly family, and His appearance and actions were so similar that His neighbors had difficulty in accepting His divinity, seeing Him only as "Joseph's son." It was not until He began to perform His mighty miracles that people were able to see Him as more than just a prophet.

B. His Limitations

1. God in Human Flesh

The Greeks had developed a religion which included deities who were claimed to be "immortals" or fully divine and deities who were produced by union of the "immortals" with mortals, producing lower levels of divinity. There is none of this concept to be found in the Bible record of Jesus' birth and life. He was God living in human flesh. He knew hunger and thirst. He knew weariness and pain, and was tempted in all points as are all men (Hebrews 4:15).

1. His Purpose

Why would God send His Son to live in human flesh, to suffer human sufferings and pain, and to die a human death? Consider the fact that God cannot die — He is eternal. Only in human flesh could Jesus fulfill the mandates of redemption and die the death which purchased our salvation. He also lived in the human condition to show us how to live — to be our example that we might follow "in His steps."

C. Human Identity
1. The Son of Man

Over and over throughout the Gospels, Jesus referred to Himself as the "Son of man." He sought identity with mankind. He emphasized his humanness. Some have deduced from this that the concept of divinity was given to Jesus by others and not by Himself. However, there are many proofs throughout the Gospels that Jesus recognized His divinity fully. Yet to minister to the needs of sinful man, He recognized the importance of identity with man.

2. The Loving Physician

When Jesus took occasion to fellowship and eat with sinners, the Pharisees criticized Him severely (Matthew 9). He responded by reminding them that it was sick people who needed a physician and not the healthy. Jesus ministered in loving tenderness to the broken hearted, the distressed and those in the slavery of sin and demonic possession.

III. His Death and Resurrection

A. His Death
1. Prophecies

There are literally hundreds of prophecies in the Old Testament which foretold the coming of Christ, and many of these told details of His death. Note the following remarkable prophecies related to this:
1. He was betrayed by a friend (Psalm 41:9)
2. He was sold for thirty pieces of silver (Zechariah 11:12)
3. The money was used for a potters field (Zechariah 11:13)

4. Judas' place to be taken by another (Psalm 109:7,8)
5. False witnesses accused Him (Psalm 27:12)
6. He was silent when accused (Isaiah 53:7)
7. He was struck and spit upon (Isaiah 50:61)
8. He was crucified for sinners (Isaiah 53:12)
9. His hands and feet were pierced (Psalm 22:16)
10. He was given gall and vinegar (Psalm 69:21)
11. He prayed for His enemies (Psalm 109:4)
12. His side was pierced (Zechariah 12:10)
13. Soldiers cast lots for His clothes (Psalm 22:18)
14. No bones were broken (Psalm 34:20)
15. He was buried with the wealthy (Isaiah 53:9)

2. Fulfillment

When we consider the details of our Lord's death covered by prophecies given hundreds of years before His birth, we understand more of the wonderful plan of God to redeem fallen man. No other event in all of history was so fully foretold and so perfectly fulfilled. And when we consider that the price of His betrayal was most likely taken from that part of the Temple treasury which provided for sacrificial animals, we understand how completely God provided for our redemption through the sacrificial death of Christ. Every prophecy which related to Christ's first coming was fully and wonderfully fulfilled in His life, death and resurrection.

B. His Resurrection

1. The Necessity

There are some who would call Jesus Christ a martyr. Had He not risen from the dead, He would have been one. His resurrection was the confirmation of the divine plan. It confirmed His divinity

BASIC BIBLE TRUTH

and His authority. We see how important this fact was for the Early Church by the number of references to the resurrection in the New Testament writings.

2. The Purpose

The Apostle Paul called the resurrection the "firstfruits of them that slept" (1 Corinthians 15:20). He declared that it was the hope of our own resurrection, confirmed by Christ's resurrection, that made the Christian life worth living (1 Corinthians 15:19). The resurrection is our proof that we too shall rise from the dead.

3. The Implications

Not only does the resurrection of Christ confirm our own resurrection, it emphasizes the truth that we are serving a living Saviour who is able to fulfill His promises to be with us perpetually (Matthew 28:20). No other religion can point to an empty tomb where the founder has risen from the dead. He is alive and because He lives, we too shall live.

IV. His Offices

There are three offices established by our Creator to serve the needs of man: Prophet, Priest and King. There were men who served as both prophet and king (David) and others who served as prophet and priest (Samuel), but only Jesus fulfilled all three roles.

A. Prophet

1. God to Man

The role of the prophet is to reveal the message of God to man. It is a vital role and the prophets were respected in Israel, even when their message was ignored. In His prophetic role, Jesus represented the Heavenly Father speaking to man.

2. His Infallible Words

The proof of the authority of the prophet was established by whether his prophecies were fulfilled. Jesus spoke a number of prophecies which were fulfilled in great detail, such as those related to His rising from the dead and those related to the destruction of the Temple.

B. Priest

1. Man to God

The first of the divinely-given offices for men was that of the priest. In the beginning, the father held the role of priest for the family. Later, God chose men such as Melchizedek (Genesis 14). With the establishment of Law, God established a priesthood, and the priests were intermediaries between God and man, but they represented man before God.

2. Fulfillment of Calvary

Jesus is not only our High Priest, but He is also the Lamb of sacrifice. The priest of the Temple offered a lamb—Jesus offered Himself as the worthy Lamb. His death fulfilled the sacrificial requirements of the Law, as witnessed by the rending of the veil of the Temple. There is no need of a human priest to stand between us and God, for Jesus is our High Priest, ever interceding for us before the Father.

C. King

1. Man to Man

The king was given to mediate the problems between men. At first, God established a system of government whereby He chose judges who would be His champions in battle and His representative in justice between men. With the establishment of the kingdom, the king became the judge, and like Solomon, righted the wrongs done among citizens. Jesus not only brings the Heavenly Father's message to man and represents men before the Father, but He also becomes the mediator between brethren, and His love and example rights the wrongs of the human condition.

The world of the Early Church was filled with inequities and social injustices. The Church did not preach against these, but rather, preached the redeeming love of Christ and when men began to follow Christ, the injustices were righted and society was changed for the better. This is still God's way, even though the full justice of our Lord's reign will not be known until He reigns as King of kings and Lord of lords.

2. Royal Lineage

The Gospels of Matthew and Luke emphasize the royal and priestly lineage of Jesus. He was of the Tribe of Judah and of the family of David. He is called a priest after the order of Melchizedek, or a priest who is serving by divine appointment rather than Aaronic succession. In fact, by the time of Jesus' life on earth, the lines of the high priesthood had become so muddled and inconclusive that the office had become a political tool rather than a sure succession.

3. Character of the Kingdom

Jesus taught that His kingdom was not an earthly kingdom, but rather one established in the hearts of men. When we make Him Lord of our lives, we establish the kingdom within us. And those who make Him Lord of their lives will one day share in His coming kingdom upon this earth.

D. Attorney
    1. The Concept

The Word teaches that Jesus also serves as a legal representative for men in the courts of Heaven (1 John 2:1). On our behalf, He asked the Father to send the Holy Spirit (John 14:16). He makes intercession for all to come to the Father by Him (Hebrews 7:25).

    2. The Purpose

When a citizen desires to be heard before a court, he must approach the court through a representative who has standing before that court. Not all attorneys are licensed to practice before all courts. And few citizens are competent or legally qualified to represent their own interests before the courts of our lands. How much more must we have proper representation before the courts of God. In Christ, we have the best—in fact, the only attorney who can represent us before the Father.

V. Errors and Alternative Beliefs

A. Christian Science

Christian Science, and founder Mary Baker Eddy taught that Christ was "the divine idea." They do not believe in a divine trinity, or that Jesus, as a man, was divine. They say that "Jesus represented Christ, the true idea of God."

B. Mormonism

Mormonism teaches a confused concept of God. They state that God the Father is Adam, who was "celestial" and that it was Adam who caused the conception of Mary and not the Holy Ghost. They also teach that Jesus had multiple wives, including Mary, Martha and Mary Magdalene.

C. Jehovah's Witnesses

The entire idea of a divine Trinity is denied by Jehovah's Witnesses and they teach that Jesus was one of the "spirit creatures" who lived with God and who came and lived a perfect life. They teach that Jesus was an archangel before His earthly incarnation. They teach that Jesus was resur- rected in spirit only and that His body ramains on the altar of God.

D. Liberal Theology

There is a wide diversity of teachings concerning our Lord which range from the idea that He was a good man and a good example to the suggestion that we cannot be certain that He ever lived on earth. Modernists reject the idea of blood atonement and look at Jesus as a good man who became a martyr. They reject the resurrection and any theology of a second coming. They deny the virgin birth of Jesus and seek natural explanations for the miracles, which they also deny.

Questions for Review:

1. Where does the New Testament confirm the pre-existence of Christ?
2. In what way did demons confirm the deity of Christ?
3. What actions of Jesus Christ confirmed His deity?
4. In what ways do we see the humanity of Christ demonstrated?
5. Why did Jesus identify Himself so thoroughly with humanity?
6. Is there any salvation possible without the shedding of blood?
7. What events show the prophetic role of Jesus?
8. How does our Lord serve as our High Priest?
9. How and where does Jesus reign today?
10. What significant truths related to our Lord do modernists reject?

6

SALVATION

Outline

I. Means of Salvation
   A. The Old Covenant
      1. Priesthood
      2. Sacrifices
      3. Obedience Required
   B. The New Covenant
      1. Our High Priest
      2. The Price Paid
      3. Obedience Required
II. Meaning of Salvation
   A. Three Aspects
      1. Conversion
      2. Continuation
      3. Consummation
   B. Relationships
      1. To the Heavenly Father
      2. To Jesus Christ
III. The New Man
   A. Transformation
      1. Regeneration

The young Christian, eager to witness for Christ, asked a man: "Sir, have you been saved?" The man replied, "I don't remember having been lost." Salvation is an important subject and there are many ideas and theories regarding this. Our purpose here is to study what the Word of God teaches about salvation. Any understanding of this subject must begin with the knowledge that man, apart from Christ, is estranged from God. Sin breaks all communion with God and we are isolated by our sinfulness. "The wages of sin is death," wrote the Apostle Paul to the Romans, "but the gift of God is eternal life through Jesus Christ our Lord" (Romans 6:23). That gift is the wonderful response God has made to man's guilt.

I. Means of Salvation

A. The Old Covenant

When Adam and Eve sinned in the Garden of Eden, God killed an animal to make clothing—a hiding for their nakedness and an early intimation of the central theme of all of God's redemptive covenants—blood. What began at Eden was reinforced by Noah following the Flood (Genesis 8:20). Then with the establishment of the covenant with Abraham, God organized and codified His covenant requirements.

    1. Priesthood

During Abraham's life, there existed a priesthood as represented by Melchizedek (Genesis 14:18), but the rules and regulations for an established priesthood began with the selection of Moses' brother, Aaron, to be the first High Priest and the selection of the tribe of Levi to be the source for all priests. The role of the priest was that of an intermediary between God and man. The experiences at Mount Sinai demonstrate graphically the inability of sinful man to approach the holy presence of God. The priests were appointed by divine mandate. God ordered the selection process and demanded that these priests fulfill careful requirements regarding both their personal bodies and their patterns of living. The priests were set apart, or sanctified, as holy to God. No man came to God except through the office of the priests.

    2. Sacrifices

Not only did God institute a priesthood and a High Priest to stand between God and man, He also instituted a clear requirement for sacrifices on behalf of the people. When the Tabernacle was

114

built, it included a great altar where sacrifices were offered to God on behalf of the people. For sins, the people were to provide animals and on the Day of Atonement, special sacrifices were offered on behalf of the entire nation. The pattern of redemption was rigid. It taught men that apart from God's provision, man was a slave to sin and estranged from his Creator. The Mosaic Law provided a pattern whereby people could come again into fellowship with God. No alternatives were provided. No other ways were accepted. Only by coming according to the provisions of the Law could sinners find acceptance by God.

3. Obedience Required

When God put the rituals and procedures in place for Israel, the third element of redemption was required — obedience. For men to find acceptance from God, they must come to the priest, must provide a sacrifice and must obey the plan given by the Lord. The existence of the priesthood and the fact of the altar of burnt offerings alone would not redeem. The people were required to be obedient to the plan God had instituted.

The Word of God teaches that this Law was a "schoolmaster" to bring men to Christ (Galatians 3:24). In type and shadow, the provisions of the Law foreshadowed the reality of Calvary and the wonderful plan which God had intended from the foundation of the world. To bring this into effect, however, required the establishment of a new contract or "covenant" between God and man. This is why Jesus said to the disciples in the Upper Room, "this is my blood of the new testament [covenant], which is shed for many for the remission of sins" (Matthew 26:28).

B. The New Covenant

Just as the old covenant or testament required a priesthood and a sacrifice, so did the new. Consider how wondrously the old covenant foreshadowed the coming of Jesus Christ, and the plan of salvation which would be purchased by His sacrifice.

1. Our High Priest

The book of Hebrews stresses that the new covenant is a better covenant. The writer appeals to Psalm 110:4 to show that Jesus did not need to come from the Tribe of Levi to serve as our eternal High Priest — His priesthood is after the "order of Melchizedec." He is called the "High Priest of our confession" (3:1), the "priest of good things to come" (9:11) and "great high priest" (4:14). Jesus fulfills to perfection the role of intermediary between God and man. He sits at the right hand of the Father. He is our "advocate" or legal representative. He is a perfect High Priest, without sin or imperfection. He has earned the right to represent every sinner who comes to God and to bring that sinner into God's redeeming grace.

2. The Price Paid

The price of redemption has always been blood. "Almost all things are by the law purged with blood; and without shedding of blood is no remission" (Hebrews 9:22). On the annual Day of Atonement, the High Priest would offer a spotless lamb as the sacrifice for the sins of all men. When Jesus hung on the cross of Calvary, He was the "Lamb slain from the foundation of the world" (Revelation 13:8). When our Saviour cried: "It is finished," the price of our redemption was paid.

A beautiful and illustrative story is told of the small boy who made a boat, and who loved it greatly and was so proud of it. While sailing it in a small ditch one day, the boat entered a swifter stream and was swept from his sight. He grieved for it; but walking down the street one day, he saw his boat in a store window. He went in and asking the price of the boat, paid it. As he walked away with the little boat clutched lovingly in his arms, he said: "Little boat, you are twice mine. You were mine because I made you, and now you are mine because I bought you!" God made us, but we were lost in trespasses and sins. Then Jesus paid the price of our redemption on the cross and we are twice His — His because He made us and His because He bought us with His own precious blood.

The sacrifices of the Law demanded that the paschal lamb be without spot or blemish. The Temple kept a special treasury for purchasing this sacrificial lamb. It is believed that it was from that fund the High Priest took the thirty pieces of silver to pay Judas for the betrayal of Christ. The paschal lambs of ancient days sufficed for a season, but every year, and often between times, the people had to bring a new sacrifice to the altar. When Jesus offered Himself as the spotless Lamb of God, He satisfied the requirements of Heaven for all time. The price is paid, and it is enough to redeem the vilest sinner. It is interesting that the first person to be saved by the blood of Jesus was a thief suffering the death penalty for his crimes.

It defies all logic that the symbol of suffering and execution should be the symbol of glory for Christendom. Can you imagine glorifying an electric chair, a guillotine or a gas chamber? Yet the cross was the instrument of taking life — of capital punishment. But because of what the cross means it has become the object of glory. Paul cried, "God forbid that I should glory, save in the cross of our Lord Jesus Christ" (Galatians 6:14). The blood washes away the sins of the repentant sinner who comes to Christ. Jesus taught us, by means of the sacrament of communion, to remember His death and to understand the awful price He paid for our redemption.

3. Obedience Required

The availability of redemption alone is not sufficient. Under the Law, there were cities of refuge where the citizen threatened with retaliatory death could flee for refuge. The city, however, never came to the man—he had to go to the city. Likewise, the endangered citizens could go to the Temple grounds and take hold of the "horns of the altar" and no man could harm him while he held to these. The house of God was a place of safety if the citizen would obey the teachings of the Law. Likewise, the salvation which Christ has purchased with His blood will avail only if we obey what has been commanded. The beautiful John 3:16 verse shows that the call is for "whosoever," but believing is also required. In other texts, we are told to believe on the Lord Jesus Christ, and to confess with our mouths that He is our Lord and Saviour. Obedience will bring us to Christ and obedience will enable us to serve Him faithfully and well.

II. Meaning of Salvation

A. Three Aspects

There are areas of confusion within the Church regarding just what we mean by the word "salvation." What appears to be disagreement is often more a matter of word meanings. Here we will define the three aspects of salvation as taught in the Word of God.

1. Conversion

To accept Christ as Saviour is indeed a simple act. It requires our acknowledging that He is Lord and that He died for our salvation. When we ask Him to forgive our sins and to take us as His child, we speak of it as being "saved." Because we use this same word to describe other aspects of our journey to Heaven and others use the same word in different ways, we need to define what we mean. In recent years, the word "born again" has been popularized and misused by some. Jesus told Nicodemus that He must be born again in order to have eternal life. This simple concept confounded that brilliant scholar. Yet when we accept Christ through repentance and faith, our names are written in the Lamb's book of life, and we become children of God. The miracle which takes place is like no other experience. Salvation is by faith, and not by works (Ephesians 2:8). We pass from death into life (John 5:24). Our names are written in the book of life (Philippians 4:3). We are brought into the family of God (Romans 8:17).

2. Continuation

The Bible also makes clear that walking with the Lord is necessary to the ongoing or continuing Christian experience. Obedience is necessary to conversion and it is necessary for continuation of our relationship. "For as many as are led by the Spirit of God, they are the sons of God" (Romans 8:14). Jesus said, "If a man love me, he will keep my words" (John 14:23). Once we have repented of our sins and accepted Jesus Christ as our Lord and Saviour by faith, we must strive to walk in obedience to the Lord. This ongoing walk is vital to our continuing relationship with Christ.

3. Consummation

The blessed assurance that Jesus is our Saviour helps us to walk in obedience to the Lord. Yet temptations come because it is possible to deny our Lord or to turn away from the faith. The Apostle Paul could proclaim with justifiable joy: "I have fought a good fight, I have finished my course, I have kept the faith" (2 Timothy 4:7). It is because he could face the end of his life after faithfully following the Lord that he had the assurance of a crown of life. Jesus taught that a man who put his hand to the plow and turned back was unworthy of the Kingdom of God. Paul taught that the crown was to the one who completed the race (1 Corinthians 9:24). In the message to the seven churches of Asia (Revelation 2:1-3:22), the rewards are promised to those who are the overcomers—the ones who finish the race.

B. Relationships

Under the old covenant, God established a special relationship with the children of Israel. This covenant was limited by national blood, but there were provisions made for those who wished to become Jewish and thus, to inherit the covenant blessings. God spoke of this relationship as a marriage and accused the nation of being estranged from Him. He called them His children on other occasions. Differing human relationships were used to illustrate the close relationship which God wanted with men, but the faithlessness of the Jewish nation made it impossible for God to establish the working relationship which He really desired. Under the new covenant, we are brought into the very family of God and are made heirs of God and joint heirs with Jesus Christ (Romans 8:17).

It is one thing to be brought into communion with God and quite another to be brought into this very close relationship. Jesus presented God as our loving Heavenly Father. We are His children and enjoy all the rights and privileges of this relationship when we are redeemed through the blood of Jesus Christ. One of the most challenging verses in the Bible is: "Let this mind be in you, which was also in Christ Jesus: who, being in the form of God, thought it not robbery to be equal with God . . ." (Philippians 2:5,6) This does not imply that there is equality between men and God, but it does illustrate the Heavenly Father's desire to be close to His children and to infuse their minds with His divine thoughts.

2. To Jesus Christ

Our relationship with our Lord Jesus Christ is illustrated in a variety of ways. Christ called His followers His brethren and this is further demonstrated by the fact that we are made joint heirs with Him in God's promises. We are also likened to branches which are firmly rooted in the vine, from which the branches draw their very life. He is our Lord, and must be given pre-eminence in our lives. Yet His rulership is benevolent, indeed. He is no slavedriver or manipulator. He rules in order to bless us. The relationship can only be illustrated by such human examples, for the tie which binds our hearts to Jesus Christ is unique and wondrous.

III. The New Man

The Word teaches that salvation makes us new creatures. "Therefore, if any man be in Christ, he is a new creature: old things are passed away; behold, all things are become new" (2 Corinthians 5:17). What does this mean to the believer?

A. Transformation

"Be not conformed to this world: but be ye transformed by the renewing of your mind, that ye may prove what is that good, and acceptable, and perfect, will of God" (Romans 12:2). Salvation is a transforming, or changing, experience. This miracle has astounded men since Calvary.

1. Regeneration

The transformation which takes place through God's Spirit is a total renewal or re-creation. This is what is meant by regeneration. Transform means to change the very character of a thing or a being. To regenerate is to create anew. The long list of miracles of regeneration constantly affirm the wonder of this miracle. That God could take a degenerate and through the power of the blood of Christ, make him an overcoming, victorious Christian is beyond belief, but it happens with great frequency. This is what is meant by the new birth—to be born a new creature in Christ. Old things pass away. All things are made new.

2. Justification

To be justified has been explained as being "just as if I'd" never sinned. We talk about forgiving and forgetting, but this isn't human. The mind of man never truly forgets. Yet the Bible teaches us that God removes our sins as far as the East is from the West (Psalm 103:12). They are cast into the sea (Micah 7:19). God truly forgives and forgets and removes our sins so far that they will never again be held against us. This is justification. This is the miracle whereby the sinner is made righteous.

B. New Nature

1. The Old Man

Paul spoke of "putting off the old man" (Ephesians 4:22, Colossians 3:9). There is a principle involved here which we should understand. While God provides the power to become the sons of God (John 1:12), there is an effort required on our part. We are to "put off" the old man—to crucify him—to die daily. Those who are constantly troubled by the old nature need to learn the lesson Paul would teach us. Christian maturity is the result of making right responses to the problems of life. We must actively pursue the life of holiness and obedience, trusting in the Lord's enablement to undergird our efforts. We cannot do it without Him, but He will not do it without our efforts.

2. The New Man

The Bible teaches that God has a wonderful array of miracles for the new believer. He is given a new heart (Ezekiel 18:31), a new spirit (Ezekiel 11:19), a new song (Psalm 40:3) and new mercies (Lamentations 3:23). He drinks new wine (Acts 2) and speaks with new tongues (Mark 16:17). He is promised a new name (Revelation 2:17) and will sing a new song (Revelation 14:3) when he enters that new home which God is preparing and which will inhabit a new earth, overshadowed by a new heaven! And all of this happens because he is brought into the new covenant with the Lord.

IV. Security of the Believer

One of the most fervent debates in Christianity over the last four centuries has dealt with the security of the believer. When Martin Luther brought the first successful movement toward faith in Jesus Christ as the basis of salvation, men began to examine the Bible for insight into just what were the dimensions of our relationship with God. Many elements of this discussion had been encountered centuries earlier in the Church, but the effects on world evangelization were to flow out of the Protestant Reformation.

A. Calvinism

John Calvin lived from 1509 to 1564 and fathered a significant part of the total Protestant Reformation. The reforms of Luther were advanced to a considerable degree in Germany by the time John Calvin became interested. Calvin was a scholar and in developing his theo-logical system, he sought to answer the philosophical question of why a good God would allow bad things to happen to good people. He seized on the Bible references to election and predestination, and built a system around this which provided the following five-point foundation:

Total depravity of all men
Unconditional election apart from human merit
Limited atonement
Irresistible grace
Perseverance of the saints

This five-point approach, which forms the acrostic "TULIP," is at the heart of Calvinism. He taught that all men were totally depraved because of Adam's sin. Whether a man can be saved or not is entirely in God's hands, who elects or predestines certain men to be saved and all others to eternal death. With this understanding then, it is necessary that Calvinism believe in a limited atonement, which is available only to the elect. Then the irresistible grace will assure the salvation of all the elect. The final point is consistent with that position and states that the saints will be saved, no matter what happens. The Puritans who settled America were Calvinistic in their theology. The Presbyterians who evangelized Scotland under John Knox were likewise Calvinists. A considerable portion of all Protestants are influenced by the teachings of John Calvin.

2. Relationship to Redemption

Under Calvinism, there remains a serious question about the right of Christians to evangelize others or to promise redemption to those who may not be among the elect. The early Calvinists believed that no man could truly know that he was saved, but if he was able to live a good life, it was at least an indication that he might well be among the elect of God.

125

3. Problems of Calvinism

Even though Calvin taught the importance of living a good and moral life, the very concept of the theology encourages laxity. Evangelism is of questionable merit if you hold to strong Calvinistic views. Of course, not all who hold to Calvin's theology carry it to the ultimate limits, but the emphasis on divine election and the perseverance of the saints has taken the elements of salvation totally out of the hands and the will of man and placed it in the hands of what appears to be an arbitrary God.

B. Arminianism

The proponents of Calvinism popularized congregational forms of church government and spread the Gospel into many lands, influencing a significant element of the total Protestant Reformation. However, the extreme limits to which some carried the doctrines brought a reaction from a Dutch leader, James Arminius (1560-1609).

1. Answer to Calvin

James Arminius did not disagree totally with John Calvin, but he saw problems with many of the views taught by him and his followers. He saw Calvinism as making God the author of sin and man as an automaton robbed of his will and any control over his own destiny. He found this abhorrent and taught that man could be drawn of the Holy Spirit to God and that the grace of God would enable a man to cooperate in working out his own salvation. His teaching was that election was conditional rather than unconditional.

2. Predestination vs Free Will

The teachings of Arminius were passed to the Church through elements of the Anglican church, the Methodist revival and the Salvation Army. Many of the more evangelical churches stress man's free will—the right of every man to come to Christ through the blood of Calvary. There are Bible references which are difficult to accept if you take the full Calvinistic view. The Golden Text of the Bible, John 3:16 offers eternal life to "whosoever will." If God was not willing that any should perish (John 3:17), then how could He predestine that vast numbers of people will have no opportunity for salvation? These are the questions which have brought so many to a more central position, balancing God's free grace and the sovereignty of God.

One solution to the problem of God's foreknowledge and His sovereignty is offered by the young convert who was confronted by a Calvinist. "You don't believe in election," challenged the Calvinist. "O yes, I do!" countered the believer. "I believe that there was a vote taken as to whether I would be saved or be lost. Jesus voted that I would be saved, and the devil voted that I would be lost. I cast the deciding vote!" If God's foreknowledge deprives men of the exercise of their free will, then we must assume that God chooses to limit His foreknowledge so that we might exercise that will. One explanation of predestination is that God has predestined that if we make a certain decision, appropriate results will follow. He also predestines that if we make a different choice, different consequences will result. The decision is ours, but the results are predestined.

C. How Secure are We?

There are sincere believers who teach that any man who accepts Christ as Saviour will thereby be eternally saved and cannot fall away. These rest heavily on such scriptures as John 10:28,29: "I give unto them eternal life; and they shall never perish, neither shall any man pluck them out of my hand. My Father, which gave them me, is greater than all; and no man is able to pluck them out of my Father's hand." We should notice, however, that the danger here is from outside influences.

Paul asks, "Who shall separate us from the love of Christ?" (Romans 8:35). He goes on to state that trials, principalities and powers and things past, present or future are incapable of breaking our relationship with Christ. "We are more than conquerors through him that loved us." But how do we balance this with Paul's statement that he kept his body under, lest after preaching to others, he himself become a castaway? (1 Corinthians 9:27). Revelation 3:5 certainly teaches that a name may be blotted out of the book of life.

Is there a conflict between these passages? Is Paul wrong when he states that walking after the Spirit of God is necessary for the believer to retain his relationship with Christ? The solution is found in the relationship as taught by Christ. In John 15, Jesus sets forth the truth that we are in Him as a branch is to a vine. If the branch bears fruit, it will be pruned so as to bear more fruit. However, if the branch fails to bear fruit, then it will be removed (verse 2). If our calling and election are out of the control of our wills, then why did Peter instruct us to "give diligence to make your calling and election sure: for if ye do these things, ye shall never fall." (2 Peter 1:10).

While God will not make us go to Heaven whether we want to or not, we should also understand that our salvation is not fragile. A failure does not mean that we are backslidden. The enemy loves to convince young believers that the first failure proves that they cannot live the Christian life. Such is not true. John wrote: "My little children, these things write I unto you, that ye sin not. And if any man sin, we have an advocate with the Father, Jesus Christ the righteous: and he is the propitiation for our sins" (1 John 2:1,2). To backslide is to abandon our faith and renounce the Lordship of Christ. There is security for the believer and it is in maintaining our relationship with Christ. His grace is sufficient to every need. He will not allow a trial beyond our ability to stand. We can go to Heaven if we really want to do so.

V. Errors and Alternative Beliefs

A. Spiritism

Spiritism teaches that any idea of atonement is immoral and the product of deranged imagination. They deny that there is any evidence of a fall of man into sin. Since spiritism is so often associated with demon activity, evidences abound of violent reactions to any mention of the blood of Christ in a spiritist meeting or a seance.

B. Christian Science

Mary Baker Eddy, founder of the Christian Science cult, taught that one sacrifice could never pay the debt of sin. She further taught that the blood of Christ had no power to bring forgiveness for sins. The most basic tenets of belief for Christian Science denies the existence of evil. Sin is considered a degree of insanity.

C. Jehovah's Witnesses

Charles Russell, founder and guiding light of the Jehovah's Witnesses, taught that the ransom of Jesus Christ is no guarantee of everlasting life. Instead, the witnesses teach that men will be given an opportunity during the "millennium" to cleanse themselves and come into a right relationship with God.

D. Roman Catholicism

Romanists believe in the deity of Christ. They believe that He died to save men from their sins, but their historical doctrinal development places responsibility for redemption on a relationship with the church and following of the teachings regarding the sacraments. It is a salvation of works and not of faith. Faith is founded in the church, rather than in Christ. While that is the historical position of Catholicism, there are many adherents in our day who are interpreting the Bible for themselves and accepting salvation by faith in the shed blood of Jesus Christ. It is encouraging to see the Roman Catholic church now receive some of the reforms for which Martin Luther fought and for which he was persecuted.

Questions for Review

1. In what ways are the Old Covenant and the New Covenant similar?
2. Since Jesus was not a Levite, how can He be our High Priest?
3. What are the three aspects or dimensions of salvation?
4. What is our relationship to Christ?
5. What is the primary difference between Calvinism and Arminianism?
6. What is meant by predestination?
7. What is implied by "free will"?
8. What is the greatest danger of the "once in grace" doctrine?
9. What is meant by backsliding?
10. What does it mean to be "justified"?

7

HOLINESS

Outline

I. Holiness Defined
  A. Old Testament Concept
  1. Perfection of God
  2. Meaning of Sanctification
  B. New Testament Principles
  1. Christ, our Example
  2. Saints
  C. Two Aspects
  1. Positional
  2. Personal
  D. Two Relationships
  1. Separated From Sin
  2. Separated To God
  E. Related Concepts
  1. Sanctification
  2. Justification

II. Holiness Demanded
  A. Necessity of Holiness
  1. To Show God's Glory

2. To be Effective Witnesses
3. Not of This World
B. Holiness Provided
  1. Holiness is Attainable
  2. Sustaining Help is Provided

III. Path to Holiness
A. Total Sanctification
  1. A Common Error
  2. Holiness Involves the Total Man
B. Making of a Saint
  1. The Pruning Process
  2. Putting on Holiness
C. Role of the Holy Spirit
  1. Conviction
  2. Power
  3. Enablement

IV. Holiness and Legalism
A. The Negative Approach
B. Biblical Priorities
C. Keeping the Bible View

V. Errors and Alternative Beliefs

"Follow peace with all men, and holiness, without which no man shall see the Lord" (Hebrews 12:14). This verse has generated a lot of interest, and has troubled many people. What is this holiness which we must follow in order to see the Lord? Since the Bible teaches that all have sinned and come short of the glory of God, does this place an impossible demand on the human life?

I. Holiness Defined

A. Old Testament Concept

In Leviticus 20:7, the Lord commands, "Sanctify yourselves therefore, and be ye holy: I am the LORD your God." The two words used here, "holy" and "sanctify" are significant.

1. Perfection of God

Any idea of holiness must include a standard against which the subject is measured. The Lord repeatedly stresses that He is holy (Leviticus 19:2, 21:8; Psalm 22:3). The angels acknowledge God's holiness (Isaiah 6). It was against this standard of righteousness that the Jewish idea of holiness was measured. Holiness was to be like God and to be acceptable to God. For this to take place, the Jewish people were instructed to separate themselves and all items of worship as holy unto the Lord. Once an article was sanctified, it was not to be used except in God's service. People were sanctified by two means, by personal commitment and by ritual cleansing. Reading through the Old Testament, we find all kinds of items called holy: priestly clothing, vessels of the Tabernacle and Temple and all things designated for worship.

2. Meaning of Sanctification

Sanctification was basically separation to God, establishing the fact that the object or person was to be used exclusively for God's glory. This concept is evident in the provisions for the Nazarites. These people were to be separated to God and to live by certain vows which set them apart from other people. Samson is a notable example of this type of vow of sanctification. So long as he walked in fulfillment of his vow, he had the power and presence of God with him.

Within the system of holiness, there were provided answers to the problem of loss of sanctification. If a man touched a dead body or was defiled in any way, provision was made for his cleansing. The ritual washing which was included in the Law served to keep people pure in the sight of their God.

The two steps required for sanctification were:

1) Willing setting apart as a holy object or life for God and
2) Fulfilling of the actions designated so that God would accept the gift as holy.

B. New Testament Principles

The two aspects of holiness which prevail in the New Testament are very much based on the Old Testament foundations: separation and purity. Again, holiness must have a standard against which it may be measured. In the Old Testament, the code of purity which God provided is found in the Ten Commandments. It was by these that a man's purity or holiness was measured. When the rich young ruler came to Jesus to ask about gaining eternal life, Jesus pointed him to the Ten Commandments (Mark 10). Yet just as the Heavenly Father was held up before the Jews as an example of what holiness meant, so was our Lord Jesus Christ to become the pattern for all mankind after His incarnation.

1. Christ, Our Example

"For even hereunto were ye called: because Christ also suffered for us, leaving us an example, that ye should follow in his steps: who did no sin, neither was guile found in his mouth" (1 Peter 2:21,22). Here is the living standard. But we also are given a written standard. It is the New Testament interpretation of the Ten Commandments — that we love the Lord our God with all of our heart and our neighbor as ourselves. This brief restatement of the Decalogue becomes positive in nature. It replaces the "thou shalt not" with the command to love. In love, all the provisions of the Ten Commandments are fulfilled.

2. Saints

We find an interesting designation in the New Testament—the Saints. Who are these? Growing out of the dark ages was the idea that saints are people who lived so holy in this world that they went at death directly into the presence of God and thus, had great influence with Him. Yet in the New Testament, we find the title given to the believers. The Corinthian believers were called to "be saints" (1 Corinthians 1:2). They are called "sanctified" and yet we find the letters of Paul written to very human and immature believers. Are these the saints? Are they sanctified?

In the light of the impossible demands made by some religionists on the believer, it is vital that we understand what Bible holiness is and how we may attain it.

C. Two Aspects

1. Positional

Just as there are two standards, a written and a living one and no conflict between the two, so are there two aspects of holiness. The first has to do with a relationship. We might remember that the holy vessels of the Temple were holy primarily because of their relationship with the holy place.

We must keep in mind that the source of our holiness is in Christ. It is possible to be holy only in Him. Apart from His holiness, we might be able to live good lives, but we can never be truly holy. A branch apart from the vine is only so much dead wood. Paul repeatedly cautioned that our holiness is not in ourselves but in our relationship with Christ (Ephesians 1:3 and Colossians 2:10). In Hebrews 12:10, we are told that our chastening is for our own profit, "that we might be partakers of his holiness."

2. Personal

Our relationship with Christ, however, is not intended to be a substitute for our own holy living. The Bible references which speak of our freedom in Christ also warn lest we make that freedom a hindrance to our testimony (1 Peter 2:16 and 1 Corinthians 6:12). Freedom has its responsibilities and the believer must recognize both his responsibilities to God and to others. Paul spoke of the meat offered to idols and said that he could eat that meat with no problems of conscience, inasmuch as the idols were nothing to him. However, he would gladly forego any eating of this meat if it would be a trap or stumbling block to others. This is the kind of conscience which seeks a life of holiness.

D. Two Relationships

1. Separated From Sin

The Bible concept of sanctification involves first a removal from all that contaminates. Israel was called out of Egypt. They were called to be a "holy people," separated from the nations around them and all the influences which proved to be so deadly to their walk with God. The Lord will meet the sinner where he is, but He saves the sinner out of his sins, not in them. God cannot and will not sanctify our selfish, sinful living. We must "come out from among them" and be separate, even as God required for the Jewish nation. One of the greatest hazards for the young convert is entanglement with former activities which are questionable. The Word stresses the importance of giving verbal testimony to our conversion (Romans 10:10). Such testimony makes it easer to "burn the bridges" with the past life and undergirds our decision to walk with Christ.

2. Separated To God

If we are separated from sin and do not make a firm commitment to the Lord, we lose the second vital aspect of achieving holiness. Jesus told of the man who had a demon removed from his life, but when the demon came again, found the heart "empty, swept and garnished" and brought seven other demons worse than himself and established his abode there (Matthew 12:43-45). The act of sanctification involves both the decision to come out of the world and to follow the Lord. We are assured of God's help in accomplishing both these goals.

E. Related Concepts

1. Sanctification

We have discovered that sanctification involves separation from all unholy involvements and separation to God's service. Vessels which had been sanctified for use in the Temple could never be used for other purposes. The Levites, who had been consecrated to God's exclusive service, could not share in the divisions of the land. They were "holy unto God."

2. Justification

Holiness involves being justified before God —
standing before Him without any guilt in His sight.
From the human perspective, this is impossible.
None can live so holy in himself as to be accepted
before God. It is in Christ that we are justified
before God. Justification accomplishes the task of
making us holy before God, but we must also seek
holiness before men and that is where dedication
and seeking God's help are necessary.

II. Holiness Demanded

A. Necessity of Holiness

1. To Show God's Glory

The greatest hindrance to evangelism today is
the lack of holy living on the part of Christians.
While the charge of "hypocrisy" is often used as an
excuse by the unconvinced sinner, the carnality
which exists keeps many sincere people from
Christ. This is one of the primary purposes for the
Apostle Paul's admonitions to the Corinthian
church (1 Corinthians 10: 32). In 2 Corinthians 4,
Paul talks of the gospel "hid to them that are lost"
and speaks of the treasure in earthern vessels.
Then he sums up the responsibilities of the believer in verse 15, "For all things are for your
sakes, that the abundant grace might through the
thanksgiving of many redound to the glory of God."

2. To be Effective Witnesses

A life of dedication and holy living has tremendous impact on the world. Men are so accustomed
to seeing selfishness and self-serving that they are
inherently suspicious of anyone who talks to them
about changing their lives. When the glory of Christ

is evident in the life of the witness, it adds impact and effectiveness to the words spoken. The old adage, "What you are speaks so loud I cannot hear what you say" certainly illustrates this principle.

3. Not of This World

We are taught that Christians are citizens of another kingdom. Christ is the King of our lives and should reign as Lord on the throne of our hearts. When He is enthroned there, He will help us to live overcoming lives. When we are told to "love not the world, neither the things that are in the world" (1 John 2:15), we are encouraged to keep our loyalties in the right place. The love of worldly things and the holding of worldly attitudes will set our hearts on this world and its values. Holiness is possible only as we set our hearts on things above and not on things of this world.

B. Holiness Provided

1. Holiness is Attainable

God will never ask us to be something we are incapable of being. He will not ask us to do something we cannot do. When He demands that we be holy, He makes a way for us to accomplish this. What often stands in our way in this respect is self-righteousness. God calls this "filthy rags."

The rich young ruler assured Jesus that he had kept the commandments of God from his youth, but when asked to give his wealth to help others and to follow Jesus, he proved that he did not love others enough and he did not love God enough to follow His Son. He was self-righteous. He was not holy.

2. Sustaining Help Is Provided

The only thing a man can do to be saved is to come to Christ. No works will help him become a child of God. It is entirely by grace that we are saved. However, to walk in obedience to the Lord's instructions does take conscious effort on our part and we are taught to do this. Paul recognized the fact that his consecration must be renewed every day. "I die daily," he said, noting the importance of dying out to the flesh on a regular basis. The words of the Lord to Paul, "My grace is sufficient for thee," were significant in terms of the overcoming life. "I have overcome the world," said Jesus just before Calvary. In John 17, we see the words of Jesus to the Heavenly Father: "They are not of the world, even as I am not of the world." He then prayed that God would "keep them from the evil" (v.15) His prayer included that His followers would be sanctified. He who overcame the world will give us power to do the same.

III. Path to Holiness

A. Total Sanctification

1. A Common Error

The Early Church wrestled with a cultistic error which greatly threatened the purity of the gospel message. This error was called "Gnosticism." Essentially, the Gnostics believed that the world was divided into two realms: the spiritual and the material. This influence came from Greek philosophical roots, and became one of the most insidious errors faced by the Early Church. Gnosticism separated the spiritual side of man from the carnal and taught that if a man was "in Christ" he would be saved and whatever his physical body did was of little or no concern. Does that sound like some thinking in our own day?

The Bible teaches that we will be judged by the deeds "done in the body" (2 Corinthians 5:10). There is no Bible basis for separating the spiritual area of life from our bodily deeds. The Apostle Paul saw the necessity of bringing his body under subjection lest after preaching to others, he become a castaway (1 Corinthians 9:27).

Holiness begins in the heart, but it will work itself outwardly into our moral convictions and our personal actions. This is why the Apostle Paul dealt severely with the Corinthian church regarding sins which existed among the believers. They were instructed to purify the body of believers and to separate themselves from sin. "If any man defile the temple of God, him shall God destroy; for the temple is holy, which temple ye are" (1 Corinthians 3:17). What he means about the temple being holy is that it has been dedicated to God and thus was set apart. To desecrate the temple of our bodies will bring sure destruction.

2. Holiness Involves the Total Man

God has created us a trinity — body, soul and spirit. Each part of us is involved in God's plan for holiness. The progression of sin shown in James 1:14,15 illustrates the truth that sin begins in the mind with unholy desires. What is allowed to remain in the mind in the form of temptation will ultimately work outward into sin, and sin into death. This is why the Scriptures stress the importance of pure thoughts (Philippians 4:8). This is scriptural mental health, and it leads to purity of life and holiness in God's sight.

Holiness consists not only of the things we don't do, but involves obedience in the things which the Lord has commanded us to do. True holiness involves loving others and will make us aware of our responsibilities for other believers.

B. Making of a Saint

While holiness is not maturity, there is much which is shared by these two measures of Christian living. Maturity deals with how emotions are handled and how choices are made. Holiness involves walking in obedience to God's Word. The youngest believer can attain substantial levels of dedication and consecration to God, and walk in the revealed light while in the process of gaining spiritual maturity. The end product of sustained holiness should be spiritual maturity.

1. The Pruning Process

The Lord has not called us to live at the minimum level of spirituality. We should grow in the faith and in spiritual knowledge. Paul spoke of believers who were on the "milk" of the Word, while he had matured to a spiritual diet of "meat." As we seek new plateaus of spiritual living, we will understand what our Lord spoke of when He said: "Every branch in me that beareth not fruit he taketh away: and every branch that beareth fruit,he purgeth it, that it may bring forth more fruit" (John 15:2). For the producing believer, the Lord has promised a pruning process. The wood which the Heavenly Father cuts away from our lives is not evil or sinful wood — but it will stand between us and our duty to bear much fruit. Some of the things which the Holy Spirit will seek to cut away from our lives may not be inherently sinful, but it is a weight which will prevent us fulfilling God's perfect will for our lives. The ideal is not to see how close we can walk to the world and still get to Heaven, but to see just how close we can walk to God in order to fulfill His perfect will for our lives.

    2. Putting on Holiness

". . . that ye put on the new man, which after God is created in righteousness and true holiness" (Ephesians 4:24). Holiness is not the product of passive acceptance. We are charged with the responsibility to put on Christ — to put on the spiritual armor — to put on holiness. We cannot do this by ourselves, but God will not do it without our own effort. It is His righteousness, but it will be imparted to the earnest seeker.

C. Role of the Holy Spirit

The Holy Spirit is God's agent for drawing us into holiness. He will convict us of sin and show us what are the "weights" which so easily beset us. He will serve to prune from our lives the attitudes and actions which stand between us and God's ideal plan. "That the righteousness of the law might be fulfilled in us, who walk not after the flesh, but after the Spirit" (Romans 8:4). Verse 1 of that same chapter says that there is no condemnation to those who walk after the Spirit. In the first chapter of Philippians, Paul talked of the good thing which Christ had begun in them and pointed out that it would grow until they were "filled with the fruits of righteousness."

Is sanctification an instant act of God or is it a progressive work? Certainly there are times in the life of the sincere Christian when the Holy Spirit draws us to new levels of dedication and consecration and when the Spirit helps us to reach new spiritual plateaus. Those are precious times and to be sought. However, both in the Bible and in life, we find abundant evidence that the sanctifying work of the Holy Spirit will abound in the lives of those who follow after the Lord in continuing dedication. Both are valid and both should work together to help us reach God's ideal of holiness in our personal lives.

2. Power

One of the numerous benefits of the Holy Ghost baptism is the enduement of power from on high. This power is to witness, but it will also be a sanctifying force in our lives. Before the Pentecostal experience, Peter was vacillating and weak. After the Day of Pentecost, he was resolute and strong in Christ. We might find understanding as we view the lives of two Old Testament prophets who were filled with God's Spirit. Elijah had a mighty experience with God and could do great deeds, but he suffered from weakness of will and did not have the confidence which should mark the life of a faithful messenger of God. Elisha, his successor, sought a double portion of the Spirit and aside from the greater number of miracles, we see a man with great spiritual maturity and holiness of life. The Holy Ghost will give us power to overcome — to be more like our Lord — to walk in holiness before God and before men.

3. Enablement

With power comes the ability to do what we could never do alone. The Holy Spirit will give us power to accomplish what the Spirit directs that we should do. This enabling power will cause us to say with the Apostle, "I can do all things through Christ which strengtheneth me" (Philippians 4:13). One act of the Holy Spirit which results in holiness for God's people is in the leadership which He provides. In Ephesians 4:11,12, we see a listing of these ministries, and the three-fold results of these Spirit-provided functions, the first of which is to "perfect the saints."

IV. Holiness and Legalism

When Satan cannot get us to stop short of holiness, he will push to make us go beyond holiness into self-righteousness. If he can get us to be proud of our dedication, he will have won a major victory. Pride is not compatible with holiness. It is a sin of the flesh and can be more destructive than many of the actions we might criticize.

A. The Negative Approach

Holiness does not consist solely of what we leave off, or a style of living or dress. Some of the most evil people in the world dress conservatively and put on many of the outward attributes of holy living. Certainly holy living will affect our life both inwardly and outwardly. The true saint of God will want to show forth Christ's glory in every aspect of life. The dedicated believer will not want to dress or act in a way which will bring descredit on our Lord or damage the effectiveness of his testimony. We are responsible for how our lives affect others. However, it is important that we realize that true holiness comes from within. As it affects our outward man, it will also reflect Christ's beauty and love from within our hearts. If that inward beauty is lacking, it is vital that we go back to the altar of dedication and renew our "first love" in Christ.

B. Biblical Priorities

The Bible sets some clear priorities for the believer. We must first become a believer through accepting Christ in faith. Until that happens, all the outward changes will have absolutely no effect on our eternal destiny. When we have entered into a personal relationship with Christ, we are to begin the process of spiritual growth. This will include a hunger for spiritual things and a determination to be more and more like our Lord. We will seek identity with fellow believers and will join in fulfilling our Lord's commission to carry the gospel into all the world. This obedience will then bring us into a growing level of personal dedication and holiness. It is important that we neither break this flow toward a high level of spirituality, nor allow unscriptural attitudes to enter our hearts and thus frustrate God's will in other lives.

C. Keeping the Bible View

To hear some people talk, going to Heaven consists of what you wear and the places you don't attend. We must keep the teachings of God's Word clearly in view. If we allow our own self-righteousness to destroy a young believer, what have we gained? How often Satan convinces the immature believer that he has "arrived" spiritually, and that his new level of dedication is the minimum for all believers. That deceived one will then become the critic of all who do not measure to his own perceptions. He will criticize and belittle those who have not reached that level. We should be eager for spiritual growth and to attain higher levels of sanctification, but we must not create barriers which God himself has not set. Christianity has some minimum Bible standards, and we have no right to add to these for the new Christian. However, we have every right and a duty to grow in our own spirituality and holiness. We should seek to live by the highest standards possible. We have the right to live above minimal Christianity. But we should be careful lest our attempts to impose our own standards on others cause some weak but sincere Christian to fall away and be lost. That is a heavy load of guilt to carry to the Judgment bar of Christ.

V. Errors and Alternative Beliefs

There are a wide variety of variant beliefs related to holiness. Most cults avoid any requirements for personal holiness and seek to substitute man-made standards or requirements for this. Christian Science teaches that man is incapable of sin, so holiness would have little meaning in their system. Mormonism denies justification by faith in Christ, and makes rightness a matter of personal works. Modernists have abandoned faith in the Bible, and thus have no standard to measure holiness against. Even within the Evangelical community, there are those whose emphasis on the free grace of God through Christ causes them to place little or no emphasis on personal living. Through all of this carelessness regarding responsibility for our lives gleams the Word of God and its high moral standard. We must walk in the light of God's Word, and let its plain teachings guide us as to what is right, and what the Lord requires of us.

Questions for Review

1. What does "saint" mean?
2. Define "sanctification."
3. What two steps are required for anything to become holy?
4. What harm results when a believer fails to walk in holiness?
5. Why is holiness attractive to the sinner?
6. What is the role of the Holy Spirit in our sanctification?
7. What is the purpose in our spiritual "pruning"?
8. Will prayer alone make us holy?
9. What are the dangers of self-righteousness?
10. Why are most cults unconcerned with teaching holiness?

8

HOLY SPIRIT

Outline

I. Person of the Holy Spirit
 A. Holy Spirit in the Old Testament
  1. In Creation
  2. In Anointing
 B. Personality of the Holy Spirit
  1. Pronouns Used
  2. Demonstrated Divine Attributes
  3. Evidences of Divinity

II. Place in the Trinity
 A. Doctrine of the Trinity
  1. Old Testament Intimations
  2. New Testament Proofs
  3. Supporting Evidences
 B. Challenges to the Doctrine
  1. Historical Challenges
  2. Rulings of the Church
  3. Modern Day Challenges

III. Work of the Holy Spirit
  A. Regenerative Work of the Holy Spirit
    1. Convincing Men of Sin
    2. Drawing Men to Christ
  B. Baptism in the Holy Ghost
    1. Promised Blessing
    2. Pentecostal Fulfillment
    3. Promise for All Generations
    4. Purposes for the Baptism
    5. Evidences of the Infilling
  C. Works of the Holy Spirit
    1. Gifts of the Spirit
    2. Fruit of the Spirit
    3. The Comforter
    4. The Teacher
    5. Executive of the Godhead
  D. The Holy Spirit as Sanctifier

IV. Sins Against the Holy Spirit
  A. Sins by the Unbeliever
    1. Grieving the Holy Spirit
    2. Resisting the Holy Spirit
    3. Blaspheming the Holy Spirit
  B. Sins by the Believer
    1. Lying to the Holy Spirit
    2. Quenching the Holy Spirit
    3. Despising the Holy Spirit

V. Errors and Alternative Beliefs
  A. Christian Science
  B. Eastern Mysticism
  C. Mormonism
  D. Jehovah's Witnesses

I. Person of the Holy Spirit

With the rise of the Twentieth Century Pentecostal revival, we are seeing a corresponding rise of interest in the truths related to the Holy Spirit. In the early years of this century, there was considerable resistance toward any substantial development of these truths, primarily out of a fear of what many believers saw as a "dangerous error" in their ranks. It has been only as the impact of the revival has bridged historical and denominational lines that scholars outside the Pentecostal movements have opened their hearts and minds to the teachings of the Word of God related to these precious truths. Not every serious or honest scholar agrees on all points, but there has been an openness to the wonderful reality of a personal "Comforter" who will walk alongside the believer, and grant power for service and holiness of life.

A. Holy Spirit in the Old Testament

1. In Creation

When God first appears in the pages of the Bible (Genesis 1), we see a reference to the Spirit of God which "moved upon the face of the waters" (Genesis 1:2). This was followed by God's declaration: "Let us make man in our image, after our likeness" (v. 26). Was this an "emanation from God" or was it a divine Person? The answer to this is not easily found in the Old Testament, but we do find the Spirit with a voice and other attributes of personality there.

2. In Anointing

One of the primary acts of the Holy Spirit in the Old Testament involves the anointing which rested on certain people. The Spirit of God rested on

Moses (Numbers 11:17), and was placed on others (Numbers 11:26). The Judges experienced such an anointing (Deuteronomy 34:9; Judges 3:10; 11:29; and 13:25). In the early years, the kings of Israel were anointed of the Spirit (Saul, 1 Samuel 11:6; and David, 1 Samuel 16:13). The prophets were anointed in special measure for service, and we are inspired by the example of Elisha who asked a double portion of God's Spirit to rest on himself.

B. Personality of the Holy Spirit

1. Pronouns Used

While the Holy Spirit is given neuter gender in the Scriptures, there are abundant evidences that the Holy Spirit is a Person. He has emotions and feelings—can be grieved and be the object of lies. The use of "It" or "Itself" relating to the Holy Spirit have misled some people. In the 16th chapter of John's Gospel, we see the pronoun "He" used repeatedly of the Holy Spirit. The Greek word, "pneuma," is used of the Spirit and would be neuter gender in ordinary usage, for it can also be translated "wind." However, the Bible used a masculine form of this in 1 John, denoting the divine person of the Holy Spirit. Other actions of the Holy Spirit show that He is a divine Person, directing and enabling the Church.

2. Demonstrated Divine Attributes

The Holy Spirit is divine, as attested by His actions throughout the New Testament. He is called God (Acts 5:4). He shares in God's eternal existence (Hebrews 9:14), His omnipresence (Psalm 139:7-10) and his omniscience (1 Corinthians 2:10,11). He is associated with the Father and the Son in the baptismal formula.

3. Evidences of Divinity

Jesus stressed the importance of respect for the Holy Spirit when He taught that it was an unforgivable sin to blaspheme the Spirit. We see repeated occurrences of miracles attributed to the power of the Holy Spirit throughout the Book of Acts. In fact, it has been suggested that the most accurate name for that book would be: "Acts of the Holy Ghost." The book is a remarkable record of the Holy Spirit working with men to accomplish the will of the Heavenly Father.

II. Place in the Trinity

A. Doctrine of the Trinity

1. Old Testament Intimations

You will not find any specific mention of a Trinity in the Old Testament, but you will find intimations of its existence. In the act of creation, we find a suggestion of multiple personalities as God speaks to say "Let us make man" and the Holy Spirit hovers over the waters. While this is not a conclusive proof of the existence of the Trinity, there is no inconsistency between the revelations of God in the Old Testament and the New Testament teachings of the existence of a Trinity. The plural form of God's name, Elohim, also supports this, as do the references to the "Angel of the Lord" who has divine attributes throughout the Old Testament and is thought to be the pre-incarnate Christ, who was with God in the beginning, and is God (John 1).

2. New Testament Proofs

The New Testament clearly teaches the existence of a Godhead — a Trinity of three Persons who exist in perfect unity, but each of whom fulfills a specific part in the purposes of God. In the New Testament, we see such clear evidences as Christ in the river of Jordan at baptism, while the Heavenly Father speaks from heaven, and the Holy Spirit descends in the form of a dove. In the formula for water baptism, Jesus taught us to baptize in the "name of the Father, and of the Son and of the Holy Ghost" (Matthew 28:19).

Additionally, we have the stated intention of Jesus to pray the Father that He would send the Comforter — proof that the three are not a corporate "one" but "trinity" or as some explain it, a "tri-unity."

3. Supporting Evidences

Jesus taught us that the Holy Spirit would testify of Him (John 15:26). This is an obvious recognition by our Lord that the Holy Spirit is separate and apart from Himself. Additionally, the Apostle Paul included all three members of the Godhead in his apostolic benediction (2 Corinthians 13:14).

With all of these and many more evidences of the Trinity, why is there a question about this? Is there credability in the assertion that we believe in three Gods?

The primary proof text for those who teach against the Trinity is found in John 10:30, "I and my Father are one." A second text appealed to is John 14:9, "he that hath seen me hath seen the Father." How do we support the teaching of the Trinity in the face of these verses? First, we must understand one significant difference between the Bible languages and the English.

We have no English equivalent of the Greek word which is a compound unity. Two examples clarify this and resolve the difficulty. First, we appeal to the words of Jesus in John 17: "That they all may be one; as thou, Father, art in me, and I in thee, that they also may be one in us" (v. 21). Were Peter and James to become a single person? No. The idea of a plural unity is further supported by the Bible teaching regarding marriage. Here, we are taught that two people will become one. One body? No, but one in love and unity. The Bible abounds in references to entire bodies of people called "one." This is the same Bible word used when God speaks of His own unity. What Christ taught was that there was so perfect a harmony between the will of the Father and the actions of our Lord that one was a perfect reflection of the other.

B. Challenges to the Doctrine

1. Historical Challenges

Within the first three centuries of Christianity, the Church faced a wide variety of heresies. Among these was a false doctrine which came to be called "Monarchianism." This took two forms, both of which have modern counterparts. The first, a forerunner of modern unitarianism, taught that there was "one God" and that Jesus was not truly divine. A second form was similar in many respects to what is popularly called the "oneness" movement of our own day. These Monarchians taught that God was revealed first in the Old Testament as a Creator, and then came in human flesh and became Christ and our Saviour. Then He returned as the Holy Spirit and thus, all three names were the same divine Person.

2. Rulings of the Church

The heresies of the Early Church age were responsible for the formation of a series of decisions which have guided the Church and have resulted in the establishment of principles of Bible interpretation. In 325 AD, the Christian Church held a council to establish an official position on matters of doctrine. There the beginnings of what was later completed as the Nicene Creed were laid. This creed was given its final form in 589 to state that the Holy Spirit, which "proceedeth from the Father and the Son," is coequal, coeternal and consubstantial with the Father and the Son. These Church leaders felt that no other view could be consistent with the total body of Bible teaching. "God in three Persons, Blessed Trinity" are the time-honored words of a favorite hymn.

3. Modern Day Challenges

There are two primary challenges to the historic position of the Church on the Trinity. First is represented by the Unitarians who teach that Christ was only a good teacher and not divine. They do not believe in Christ's resurrection, or that His teachings have more than moral or ethical value. The second, which is accepted by many sincere believers, is that there is only one personality taught in the Bible. They believe essentially that the words "in the name of" as related to water baptism are descriptive of all names used in the Bible for divine beings and that Jesus Christ is the "name of" God. They point to the words in Acts which talk of believers being baptized "in Jesus' name" and feel that this accomplishes all truth as related to the person of God. These people, often spoken of as the "oneness" believers, are given to word games to try to explain the very obvious Bible references to the separate existence of the Father, the Son and the Holy Ghost. They are vocal in their proclamations and earnest in their position, but the sure guidance of the Word of God is vital to the sincere believer. We must not play word games with the Bible. We must accept truths taught there, even while our human minds are incapable of explaining every aspect of the truths we hold. The Lord never asked us to understand it all, for God's ways are as high above our human ways as the heavens are above the earth. In faith, we can accept what God has told us is so and leave the logic to Him.

III. Work of the Holy Spirit

A. Regenerative Work of the Holy Spirit

One of the most vital ministries of the Holy Spirit in this world is to serve as God's divine Agent to bring men to Christ. The Bible offers us some insights into just what His purposes and methods are.

1. Convincing Men of Sin

Men do not want to believe that they are sinners and condemned before a just God. The human ego does not want to accept a load of just guilt, and there is no shortage of voices who would convince men that they are right and that guilt is unjustified. It is the work of the Holy Spirit to "reprove the world of sin" (John 16:8). Only as men accept the Holy Spirit's message that they are sinners are they ready to come to Christ for His forgiveness.

2. Drawing Men to Christ

Jesus taught that the Holy Spirit would testify of Him (John 15:26). People who are drawn by the Holy Spirit toward Christ, and who are made aware of their sins, will then be born of the Spirit (John 3:5). The redemption of a human soul is the result of divine teamwork.

B. Baptism in the Holy Ghost

1. Promised Blessing

On the day of Pentecost, Peter demonstrated that the events of the upper room were in fulfillment of Joel's prophecies. "This is that which was prophesied" were his words. Isaiah foretold, "Until the spirit be poured upon us from on high" (Isaiah 32:15). Joel taught that the Lord would pour out His Spirit in the last days, and showed Israel that through that outpouring the Lord would restore His glory in the world and would bring again God's blessings upon mankind.

2. Pentecostal Fulfillment

Jesus taught the importance of the Holy Ghost baptism. He wanted His followers to preach the Gospel and to evangelize the world, but He told them that they were to remain in Jerusalem until they had received the promised outpouring of the Holy Ghost. It was on the Jewish feast day of Pentecost (also called the Feast of Weeks) that this promise was fulfilled. The story is a familiar one. The disciples who had a short time earlier been victims of indecision, weakness and vacillation were transformed into blazing flames of evangelism. Gone were the weaknesses which had plagued them. They were transformed by the upper room experience, and were equipped to do what the Lord had asked them to do.

3. Promise to All Generations

There are those who claim that the fullness of the Pentecostal blessing was lost after the Early Church age. Some have pointed to 1 Corinthians 13:9-12 as indicating that tongues were needed because of the imperfections of the Early Church, and that the maturing of the Church makes these gifts of little value. A careful reading will show that Paul is talking of the ages to come when we will no longer see through a "glass darkly," but will know and understand all things as we dwell for eternity in His presence. Never were the manifestations of the Holy Ghost so needed as in this day. And as Peter tells us, the promise is "unto you, and to your children, and to all that are afar off, even as many as the Lord our God shall call" (Acts 2:39). We are heirs to the promise of God's power through the baptism in the Holy Ghost.

4. Purpose of the Baptism

The Lord did not send the Holy Spirit to establish some kind of spiritual elite. There are sound reasons for the coming of Pentecost and very good reasons why the believer should seek the infilling of the Holy Ghost. In the first chapter of Acts, Jesus teaches that the infilling will bring power to witness. Earlier He had taught that the Holy Spirit would be a Teacher, bringing all things which Christ had taught to the remembrance of the believer (John 14:26). Another vital aspect of the Holy Spirit's ministry to the believer is to be the "comforter" or *paraclete* in the Greek. This means literally "one who walks alongside," or a constant companion. Every believer needs to be "filled with the Spirit" in order to fulfill God's purpose and will in his own life.

5. Evidences of the Infilling

When the historic revival came to Topeka, Kansas, it was as a result of a Bible search to find what are the biblical evidences of Holy Ghost baptism. The conclusion reached by the students of that Bible school is the same reached by countless earnest and sincere seekers since that day. The clear evidences of the Word are that God uses a physical evidence to show what has happened to the inner man. This evidence is consistently reported everywhere in the New Testament where any significant details about an infilling are given. Typical of this is what is reported on the Day of Pentecost: "And they were filled with the Holy Ghost, and began to speak with other tongues, as the Spirit gave them utterance" (Acts 2:4). This same initial, physical evidence has demonstrated the infilling of countless believers in our own day.

The tongues shown here and elsewhere in the Word should not be confused with the Gift of the Spirit which is also tongues, but used for a totally different purpose. The tongues which are the initial, physical sign of infilling are not a message to be interpreted. This sign gives visible evidence to what has happened in the heart and life. It is not the only evidence of the infilling. There are important evidences as demonstrated by the Gifts and the Fruit of the Spirit. Yet it is God's method for proving the baptism in His Spirit. Why tongues? Perhaps because of the Bible teaching that the tongue is the most unruly member of the body and incapable of human control (James 3:5-8). When the Holy Spirit controls the tongue, it implies His control of the total man.

C. Works of the Holy Spirit

1. Gifts of the Spirit

In 1 Corinthians 12:8-10, we have the classic listing of what has been called the "nine Gifts of the Spirit." These may be divided into three logical groups to demonstrate their purposes and uses:

Information Gifts:

a. Knowledge

This is knowledge which is given by divine means. A good illustration of this is the way in which the Holy Spirit talked to Simon Peter about Ananias and Sapphira (Acts 5). Knowledge which comes as a direct gift of the Holy Spirit may be similar to knowledge gained by human means, but its source is divine and its information perfect.

b. Wisdom

Wisdom has been described as the ability to use knowledge properly. There is a divine wisdom which comes as a result of prayer (James 1:5), but this is a wisdom given supernaturally for a specific time and place.

c. Discerning of Spirits

The Bible often illustrates what it teaches, and we find a variety of illustrations of this Gift of the Spirit in action. Through the Spirit, Paul knew that the young lady who was promoting his ministry was actually possessed by demons (Acts 16). In these days when there is so great a rise in satanic involvement and occult practices, believers need to be filled with the Spirit, so that the Holy Spirit might guide us into perfect knowledge of the unseen world around us.

Communication Gifts:

d. Tongues

Here the tongues used are similar in character to the evidence of the Holy Ghost baptism, but the purposes are different. This gift is one whereby the Holy Spirit speaks in a tongue unknown to the believer to give a message to the saints. This gift was abused in the Corinthian church, and was the result of some outstanding teaching by the Apostle Paul. Messages in tongues are to be orderly, and given in order, with the interpretation expected. In fact, the burden for receiving the interpretation is placed on the giver of the message (1 Corinthians 14.5). While Paul did write to bring order into the worship of the Corinthian church, he did not discourage the gift of tongues, but rather taught its proper and orderly use.

It is clear that the use of the gift of tongues is placed under the control of the believer (1 Corinthians 14:28,32). One disorderly practice in the gift of tongues is the failure of the believer to seek the Lord's guidance regarding the timing of the message. When the Spirit gives us a message or a duty in the gifts of the Spirit, we might wisely ask, "When, Lord?" in order to make proper use of the gifts.

e. Interpretation of Tongues

This is the completion of the gift of tongues for without interpretation, the message is useless and will bring disorder or confusion to the body. In 1 Corinthians 14:5, we learn that tongues plus interpretation equal prophecy, or a divinely inspired message understood by all who hear. Then the question might be asked: "Why do the Pentecostals experience so many messages in tongues and less of prophecy?" One answer is what Paul says the purpose of tongues is—a sign to the unbeliever. Tongues, when interpreted, touch unbelievers. There are many testimonies of times when the Holy Spirit has given a message in a tongue unknown to the receiver, but understood by an unbeliever in the service. When the interpretation is correct, it is impressive and has resulted in changed lives.

One other point which deserves our attention is that the Bible calls this the gift of "interpretation" not "translation." Interpretation involves placing a message in the words of the interpreter, and these will not be a literal translation, but an interpretation, which will be influenced by the vocabulary and word patterns of the interpreter. Nowhere does the Bible equate either interpretation or prophecy with the inspired and infallible Word of God. It is God speaking, but through imperfect human vessels.

f. Prophecy

This is a gift which has been misunderstood by many. Because a large percentage of the prophetic writings in the Bible deal with coming events, we tend to think of prophecy only as related to the unknown future. And prophecy, as a gift of the Spirit, does sometimes project the future (witness Agabus in Acts 21). The Bible teaches that prophecy, as a gift of the Spirit, is essentially the same as the interpretation of a message in tongues. It is a message inspired by God and of a higher order of inspiration than is common in preaching. When the Holy Spirit speaks through the gift of prophecy, we will know the source and the nature of God's communication.

Intervention Gifts:

Three of the gifts of the Spirit are used by the Lord to intervene in the natural process of things. These are the miracle gifts — the power gifts and have been used by the Lord to confirm His Word since the Early Church first went forth in the power of the Holy Ghost to plant the Christian Church.

g. Faith

It is interesting that faith is shown both as a fruit of the Spirit and a gift of the Spirit. What is the difference? Fruit grows, and a gift is instantaneous. To all are given "the measure of faith," and we are to grow this fruit in our lives, but there are times when our own faith is inadequate to the need at hand. For this, the Holy Spirit provides a divine gift of faith — superhuman faith — to meet that need. When we recognize that this is a gift of God, and not our own faith, it will help us retain our humility and perspective.

h. Miracles

Miracles have been described as that which sets aside the normal order of things. When Paul and Silas were delivered from the prison, it was a miracle. Modern science attempts to discredit any idea of supernatural intervention in the affairs of men, but the Word of God tells us that we may have gifts of the Spirit, and among these is the gift of miracles.

i. Gifts of Healing

The wording of this particular gift is unsual and has generated much discussion as to whether the gift resides in the believer or if each healing is in fact a gift of the Holy Spirit. It would seem that there is consistency intended in all of the gifts.

They are to be given to the believer. They are to do God's work effectively in our world. Certainly there is great need for the gifts of healing in our day and the fact that there are some charlatans and false prophets claiming to have power to heal takes nothing from the need within the Church for the genuine gifts of the Spirit to operate to the blessing of mankind and the growth of the Church.

Two points should be understood from Paul's teaching to the church at Corinth. First, the gifts of the Spirit were never intended as a replacement for the more necessary attributes of love, hope and faith. Without love, all the gifts in the kingdom would avail little. It has been suggested that the "best gifts" which are to be coveted are those gifts which are most needed at the moment, and which will bring the greatest glory to our Lord Jesus Christ. Finally, Paul stressed that the gifts are a trust from the Spirit and thus, should be controlled by the mature believer so that no shame or disorder disrupts the primary mission of the Church. We must keep in mind that the giving of the gifts is in the control of the Spirit, who gives "to every man severally as he wills" (1 Corinthians 12:11). The wise use of these gifts is our own responsibility.

We should acknowledge that there are other gifts of the Spirit taught in the Word of God and while the list is open to some disagreement, we should not limit our understanding of the gifts to the nine mentioned by Paul in his letter to the Corinthian church.

2. Fruit of the Spirit

The Apostle Paul not only gave us a list of nine gifts of the Spirit, but he also furnished us with a similar list of the fruit which should grow in the life of the believer. These are found in Galatians 5:22,23. These are some of the vital, continuing evidences of the baptism in the Holy Ghost. The importance of these are the subject of much of the writings of the Apostle.

a. Love

This attribute is stressed thoughout the New Testament. It is the summation of all the Law and the Prophets. It is the glue which holds the Church together and makes our relationships within the family of God more binding than with our human families. The 13th chapter of Paul's first letter to Corinth stresses this love which is a godly and unselfish love. The dimensions of this kind of love are given there.

b. Joy

There is very little evidence of joy in the Old Testament except human joy and that which is identified prophetically with the coming salvation through Calvary. In the New Testament, the opening words are of joy. The shepherds received "good tidings of great joy." The wise men rejoiced when they saw the star over Bethlehem. When the Apostle Peter spoke of "joy unspeakable" (1 Peter 1:8), where is the source? It is in the Holy Ghost (Romans 14:17). God's Spirit will fill our lives with joy if we will allow this fruit to grow in our lives.

c. Peace

Jesus said that He would leave His peace with His followers. It is a peace which passes all understanding (Philippians 4:7). It is found through the Holy Ghost (Romans 14:17) and will grow as an abiding fruit of the Spirit if we will let it.

167

d. Longsuffering

Jesus is the supreme example of longsuffering. We learn from 1 Corinthians 13 that love is longsuffering. Spiritual maturity denotes a proper control of the emotions. It is not human to suffer long or to have great patience, but it is godly. This fruit is earnestly needed in these days of egotism and self-fulfillment.

e. Gentleness

Again our Lord is the best example of a fruit of the Spirit. He was gentle and kind. The woman taken in the act of adultery experienced this redemptive gentleness. Gentleness is not compromise. It is not weakness. It is tenderness to others in the name of the Lord. Gentleness can grow beside firmness of principle. Both are needed if we would be like our Lord.

f. Goodness

We live in a time when many people debate the fact that goodness can truly exist in a human life. Human frailty is applauded and human weakness is exalted. Yet the Holy Spirit will sanctify our lives so that we can be truly good and can demonstrate a goodness of character, which will glorify our Lord, and draw men to His side.

g. Faith

Just as faith can be a divine gift of the Spirit, so must it also be a growing fruit of the Spirit. This faith is that which grows in the heart of the sincere believer who accepts God's Word and believes His promises. It is a faith founded in God and His love and not in whether God chooses to allow our request or not. It is a faith which recognizes the sovereignty of God and allows God's will to prevail, even when it is in conflict with our own wills. It is a faith in God, and not in prayer. It is the faith which will sustain the believer and enable us, with Paul, to "keep the faith."

h. Meekness

Moses was called the meekest of men. Jesus was the perfect example of meekness. Like gentleness, meekness is not weakness. Moses could be firm in the right and Jesus could be bold in defense of the Heavenly Father's will. Meekness grows out of the Spirit-guided realization of our own humanness. The Spirit-guided temperament will include meekness.

i. Temperance

Temperance is moderation in that which is good and abstance from that which is sinful. Temperance is the moderate use of God's blessings. Selfishness demands instant fulfillment and an ever-growing level of pleasure. Temperance enables us to place limits on all the things we enjoy so that our lives are balanced and godly.

One of the lessons which we might gain from the living parable of our Lord cursing the fig tree is the importance of fruit-growing. The fig tree had leaves and appeared to be loaded with fruit, but it was a living lie. It was a promise unfulfilled. Might we not come under the same judgment of our Lord if we do not bear the fruit of the Spirit?

3. The Comforter

When Jesus walked the earth with His followers, He was their Comforter and Guide. He carried them through every discouragement and guided them through each test. He was there to furnish answers and to guide their steps into fields of service. When He was preparing for the consummation of His ministry on earth, He promised His followers "another comforter." This promised Comforter is the Holy Ghost. The Greek word used here is *Paraclete* or "one who walks alongside." The implication is plain. We can have a constant divine Companion to walk with us, to teach us, and to guide us into all truth. Our Lord's promise never to leave or forsake us is fulfilled through the coming of the blessed Comforter — the Holy Ghost.

4. The Teacher

Jesus was the Teacher. Men would say that no one had ever taught as did our Lord. Yet with His ascension, His ministry of teaching ended. It is for this reason that the Holy Spirit was promised as our Teacher, who would guide us "into all truth" (John 16:13). He is the Teacher who will interpret and explain the teachings of Christ and provide guidance in all matters of life. The teaching relationship of Bible times was that of the master teacher and the student who sat at the feet of the master to learn from every word. Thus did Mary sit at the feet of Jesus. Thus should we sit at the feet of the Holy Spirit and be taught the vital lessons of obedience to our Lord and His will.

5. Executive of the Godhead

We sometimes speak of the Holy Spirit as being the "Executive of the Godhead." By this, we mean that He is the one who does the work of God in this world. He is the One charged with the responsibilities of carrying forward the redemptive plan of God through Jesus Christ. The Holy Spirit works in a perfect harmony with the Father and the Son to bring men into redemption and to present the Church as a spotless bride to Christ at the rapture.

D. The Holy Spirit as Sanctifier

One of the greatest needs of believers is help in making and keeping our lives pure. Since He draws us to Christ and serves as God's Agent for regeneration, He helps to cleanse our lives from the moment of our conversion. Through the fruit of the Spirit, He helps us to grow in the likeness and image of our Lord. Through His teaching, He guides us into truth and helps us to avoid error. As our constant Companion, He will convict us of any wrongdoing and will lead us into repentence and new levels of dedication so that we might grow in the nurture and admonition of our Lord.

IV. Sins Against the Holy Spirit

Of the six sins against the Holy Spirit discussed here, three are those most likely to be committed by the unbeliever and three are a real danger to the believer.

A. Sins of the Unbeliever

1. Despising the Holy Spirit

Hebrews 10:29 shows the danger of despising the "Spirit of grace." This is to reject or count as of no importance the call of the Holy Spirit. It is likened to walking over our Lord, or trampling His blood under foot. It is treating holy things as unholy. There are many unbelievers who are guilty of this sin and who must change their hearts and attitudes before they can be saved. Without repentence, judgment will fall (see verses 30 and 31).

2. Resisting the Spirit

Stephen accused the Jews of resisting the Holy Ghost (Acts 7:51,52). The Holy Spirit will seek to draw the sinner to Calvary. He will tenderly plead with the heart of the unbeliever. To resist the Holy Spirit is to resist God's attempt to bring us into redemption. It is a fearful thing to resist God's love as demonstrated by the tug of the Holy Spirit on our hearts.

Jesus taught that there was only one sin which could not and would not be forgiven of men and that is the blasphemy of the Holy Spirit (Matthew 12:31,32). This is not the sin of ignorance but the sin of willful denial of the Lord's Spirit. To attribute the works of the Holy Spirit to Satan is a fearful wrong and can bear terrible consequences.

B. Sins by the Believer

1. Lying to the Holy Spirit

In the story of Ananias and Sapphira in Acts 5, we see an example of two believers who lied to the Holy Spirit. They were motivated by a desire for self-glory and a basic selfishness. They conspired to lie. They did not understand the significance of their plot and paid for their sin with their lives. Not all who are dishonest with God meet immediate judgment, but it is a fearful thing to take God and His Spirit lightly.

2. Quenching the Spirit

"Quench not the Spirit" said Paul (1 Thessalonians 5:19). To quench is to put out a fire. In the Tabernacle, the fire on the altar was to burn continuously. This was a type of the Spirit and teaches us that we must let the reviving fires of Pentecost burn in our hearts, and in our churches at all times. Some critics are quick to throw "wet blankets" on the move of the Holy Ghost. We must not be guilty of quenching His fire of revival.

3. Grieving the Holy Spirit

"Grieve not the holy Spirit of God, whereby ye are sealed unto the day of redemption" (Ephesians 4:30). The next verse demonstrates the type of attitude or action which will grieve the Holy Spirit— bitterness, wrath, anger, clamor and evil speaking. How many churches have lost their effectiveness because of division in the body. How many Christians have had their own testimonies blunted by the ungracious attitudes and words of others. God names the sowing of discord among the things which He hates most. It is a grievous sin against the Holy Spirit to be a party to gossip or any other act of discord. The Church suffers enough from the attacks from without — we do not need discord and bitterness within. It is a serious sin against the Holy Spirit to lend ourselves to such activities.

V. Errors and Alternative Beliefs

We have considered the Unitarian and the "oneness" positions within the body of this study. Therefore, we will summarize only the cultistic errors related to the Holy Spirit and the doctrine of the Trinity.

A. Christian Science

Mary Baker Eddy, founder of Christian Science, taught that the very idea of the Trinity suggested polytheism. This cult sees the trinity of "life, love and truth" as their ideal. The Heavenly Father is called the "Father-Mother."

B. Eastern Mysticism

There are differences between the numerous cults deriving from eastern mysticism, but all deny the Holy Spirit and the Trinity. Generally, they teach that God is only a high "initiate" in their scheme of reincarnation. Rosicrucianism teaches that Christ and the Holy Spirit are only highly placed reincarnations. While those cults based on Eastern mysticism use many of the same terms and titles as Christianity, they apply them in different ways and mislead people into thinking that they are close to Christian viewpoints in such matters.

C. Mormonism

The Mormons will tell you that they believe in the baptism in the Holy Ghost and in speaking in other tongues. You will find it necessary to get well beyond these words to find out what they mean. They believe that their prophets have the gifts of the Spirit and that their words are divinely inspired and are equal to the Bible in that inspiration. They teach that the Heavenly Father has a body of flesh and bones, as does Christ, but that the Holy Spirit is different from them in that the Spirit has no body and thus, is not of the same substance as the Father and the Son.

D. Jehovah's Witnesses

The Jehovah's Witness doctrine clearly denies any acceptance of the Bible teaching of the Trinity. They distort the Christian teaching related to the Trinity in order to heap ridicule on the doctrine. They deny any divinity to the Holy Spirit or that He is an intelligent person. The Holy Spirit is seen as essentially an invisible force which finds its source in Jehovah God.

Questions for Review

1. What evidences of the Holy Spirit are found in the Old Testament?
2. Why do we know that the Holy Spirit is a "Person"?
3. What ancient heresy denied the Trinity?
4. What are the modern equivalents of this error?
5. What is the Holy Spirit's Role in redemption?
6. What is the initial, physical evidence of the Holy Spirit baptism?
7. What is the function of the Gifts of the Spirit?
8. How does the Fruit of the Spirit differ from the Gifts of the Spirit?
9. Why do we call the Holy Spirit the "Executive of the Godhead"?
10. What is meant by the "Comforter"?

9

ORDINANCES

Outline

I.   Water Baptism
   A. History of Water Baptism
      1. The Jewish Roots
      2. John the Baptist
      3. New Testament Practice
   B. Meaning of Water Baptism
      1. Mark of Conversion
      2. Sharing in Christ's Death
   C. Importance of Water Baptism
      1. It is not Regeneration
      2. It is Obedience
      3. It is Important
   D. Method of Water Baptism
      1. The Act of Baptism
         a. Affusion
         b. Immersion
      2. The Formula

II. The Lord's Supper
   A. The Jewish Roots
      1. History of the Passover

     2. Symbolism of the Passover
  B. Upper Room Origins
     1. Introducing the New Covenant
     2. Defining the Symbolism
  C. Observing the Lord's Supper
     1. Frequency
     2. Meanings
       a. Catholic View
       b. Luther's View
       c. What the Bible Teaches
     3. Dangers of Misuse

III. Marriage

  A. Historical Origins
     1. Its Beginnings
     2. Its Meaning
     3. Its Importance
  B. Bible Pattern of Marriage
     1. Unity
     2. Relationships
     3. Sanctity
  C. Divorce
     1. Old Testament Practice
     2. New Testament Teachings
     3. The Church Deals with Divorce

IV. Errors and Alternative Views

  A. Christian Science
  B. Mormonism
  C. Secular Humanism

BASIC BIBLE TRUTH

I.   Water Baptism

A. History of Water Baptism
    1. Its Jewish Roots

When John the Baptist began his baptismal services on the banks of the Jordan River, he was not creating a new ceremony. He was, however, giving the old ceremony an entirely new meaning. Under Judaism, a person who wished to convert to Judaism was required to go through three ceremonies:

    1) Circumcision (for the males),

    2) Immersion in water, and

    3) Offering of a prescribed sacrifice.

To the Jews, however, water baptism was not for repentance but for ceremonial cleansing. It came from the earlier rites of washing prescribed under the Mosaic Law.

    2. John the Baptist

John the Baptist was a remarkable individual. He does not appear to have been personally acquainted with Jesus, even though they were kin. He lived in a different area and there is no record of communication between them. When he began to baptize people in Jordan, it was a baptism of "repentance" and acceptance of the Kingdom which was near at hand. The Jews had lived through centuries of disillusionment and dashed hopes. They had tried with human means to re-establish the lost glory of their nation. They longed for the promised "Anointed One" or Christ (Old Testament: Messiah).

When John began to preach and to baptize in Jordan, the people thronged to hear him and many were baptized to prepare for the One whom he promised was soon to appear. There was little in the message of John to disturb the pious Jews. The fact that so many of them had worldly views of the coming Kingdom, rather than the spiritual view explains their acceptance of John and his message. It was when Christ came and showed them the nature of the Kingdom and the cost of participation that they began to reject the words from Heaven.

3. New Testament Practice

Jesus came to be baptized by John, not because He had any sin for repentance, but in order to fulfill all righteousness and to set us an example. Some of his disciples came from the followers of John the Baptist. When the Church came into being on the Day of Pentecost, we might safely assume that the majority, if not all, of the adherents had already been baptized.

When Paul asked the believers of Ephesus about their water baptism, they declared that they had been baptized "unto John's baptism" (Acts 19:1-6). On the Day of Pentecost, Peter preached to the people that they should "repent and be baptized." Water baptism followed that sermon, and all other occasions where new believers came into the Church. When Philip preached to the Ethiopian, that new convert requested water baptism. As a missionary, Paul baptized few, but placed that duty under the pastors in each local church.

B. Meaning of Water Baptism

1. Mark of Conversion

Water baptism consistently followed conversion in the Early Church. The very act of baptism served to separate the new believer from his old life and relationships. It signified the beginning of his Christian walk, and gave testimony to the world of his change.

2. Sharing Christ's Death

The believers were taught that water baptism was a means of being buried with Christ and that coming from the water represented the new life in Christ (Romans 6:3 and Colossians 2:12). This is the most vital new meaning of water baptism as it grew out of its Jewish roots. To the Jews, baptism of the convert represented a ceremonial cleansing; but in Christ, it signifies sharing in His death on the cross and being a partaker of His resurrection. As He rose from the tomb in His glorified body, so the Christian rises from the water to symbolize his entering into a new life in Christ.

C. Importance of Water Baptism

1. It is not Regeneration

The fact that water baptism is so frequently coupled with acceptance of the Lord has led some to believe that baptism is in fact the process of conversion. This is referred to as "baptismal re-generation." Acts 22:16 is one of the verses which taken apart from other references, would seem to imply that conversion came through baptism: "Arise and be baptized, and wash away thy sins, calling on the name of the Lord." A study of the total body of references to water baptism will demonstrate, however, that salvation is through repentance and acceptance of Christ. What we should not lose sight of is that the act of receiving Christ and the act of following the Lord in water baptism are so closely entertwined in the New Testament that we cannot avoid the fact that this step of obedience is vitally important to the believer.

2. It is Obedience

Jesus taught us that we were His disciples if we did what He commanded that we do. In the Great Commission, the Lord stressed the importance of water baptism: "Go ye into all the world and preach the gospel to every creature. He that believeth and is baptized shall be saved; but he that believeth not shall be damned." Salvation is through faith — through believing — but once faith has accomplished its work, obedience demands that we be baptized in water.

3. It is Important

The Early Church placed great emphasis on water baptism. Jesus placed great importance on it and demonstrated its necessity by being baptized by John. The emphasis on salvation by faith which grew out of the Protestant Reformation has brought a de-emphasis of water baptism for some people. We must not overlook the central place this truth holds in the New Testament. We might well ask in the light of the many teachings of the Word of God, if any believer who has the opportunity to be baptized in water and neglects to do so will stand justified before God? Water baptism is not salvation, but it is vital as an act of obedience.

D. Method of Water Baptism

1. The Act of Baptism

a. Affusion

"Affusion" is a word which describes baptism by the sprinkiling or pouring of water on the head. Such form of baptism is widely practiced in some Christian churches, and its roots go far back in Church history. While the Early Church, according to most authorities, practiced baptism by immersion exclusively throughout the first two centuries except in cases of a dying person who could not be immersed, the act of baptism by affusion (sometimes referred to as aspersion) gained popularity as some accepted Christ where there was no water sufficient for immersion. Then, the later practice of infant baptism made this the only practical method for babies. The rise of the idea that no one could go to Heaven without water baptism brought about an increase in infant baptism.

b. Immersion

After centuries of using affusion almost exclusively there were some movements within Christianity to return to the New Testament pattern of water baptism. The Anabaptists were a product of one wing of the Lutheran revival and they thrived in Switzerland, stressing a return to baptism by immersion. From this early reform movement came the Baptists and Mennonites of our day. They stressed the importance of immersion and influenced much of the revival which flowed into the twentieth-century Pentecostal renewal. Some groups such as the Methodists will utilize either method, but lean toward sprinkling. Pentecostals have almost uniformly adhered to the immersionist position.

Are we right to insist on immersion as the only valid means of water baptism? Consider the following facts:

1) Throughout the New Testament, we see descriptions of water baptisms which can only be by immersion; and,
2) The symbolism of burial and resurrection are virtually meaningless when applied to baptism by affusion. Since water baptism is for

those who have accepted Christ as Saviour, the baptizing of infants is unscriptural.

2. The Formula

Jesus gave us the formula for water baptism in Matthew 28:19, "Go ye therefore, and teach all nations, baptizing them in the name of the Father, and of the Son, and of the Holy Ghost." How do we correlate this with the Acts references which speak of baptizing in Jesus' name? First, if you will study the three Acts references which use this approach (2:38; 10:48 and 16:18) you will see that these do not have consistency, and therefore, are not a formula but a fact. In Acts 8:12, we see: "But when they believed Philip preaching the things concerning the kingdom of God and the name of Jesus Christ, they were baptized, both men and women." They accepted Christ and it was their faith in Christ which brought them to water baptism.

Consider Galatians 3:27: "For as many of you as have been baptized into Christ have put on Christ." These early believers were baptized "into Christ," but we might safely assume that they followed the Lord's command and were baptized in the name of the Father, and of the Son, and of the Holy Ghost. In fact, records of the Early Church speak of believers as being baptized into Christ, but when they recorded the actual occasion, the formula given by our Lord was used. There is no conflict here. We are baptized because of our faith in Christ and into Christ, but we are baptized in the name of the holy Trinity.

II. The Lord's Supper

A. The Jewish Roots

1. History of the Passover

When the Israelites were told to prepare for their deliverance from Egyptian bondage, they were instructed to kill a sacrificial lamb and to place the blood over and on each side of the door. When the angel of death came to bring God's judgment to Egypt, the presence of the blood caused the angel to "pass over" that Jewish home. The hasty meal which God told the Israelites to eat on that occasion became the first Passover meal and when God gave the Law to Moses, He commanded the nation of Israel to observe the Passover Feast annually on the anniversary of that deliverance. The form and symbolism of that Feast was very important to the Jews, and was followed faithfully.

2. Symbolism of the Passover

The Jews ate of the Passover for centuries with little or no knowledge of why God had demanded the particular form of the Feast. First, before the Passover day arrived, the Jewish home must be cleared of any form of leaven. Leaven is a type of sin and before we can have communion with our Lord, our hearts must be purified. Then, the Passover Feast, which was usually a full meal, always included certain items and activities as a part of the observance. The meal was interspersed with readings of Jewish history and the singing of the Psalms. Included were the wine, the unleavened bread and bitter herbs, along with other elements. The unleavened bread was hidden, and before being eaten, was broken. The cup of wine, which appears to have been unfermented until long after Calvary, was to be taken at specific points in the Feast. The bitter herbs represented the suffering of slavery in Egypt.

In the traditional Passover, the unleavened bread was broken early in the meal, and a half of one of the three pieces hidden under a napkin or under the table and kept for later. The wine was taken at specific points throughout the ten prescribed functions of the meal. It appears to have been during this last part of the Passover that our Lord instituted the Lord's Supper or Communion.

B. Upper Room Origins
1. Introducing the New Covenant

In Matthew 26:28, Jesus said, "For this is my blood of the new testament, which is shed for many for the remission of sins." The word translated "testament" here literally means "covenant." To Abraham, God gave the old covenant. This covenant was a contract or agreement entered into by God and Abraham and ratified by his descendants at Sinai. That covenant made the nation of Israel God's chosen people and promised that through them all nations of the world would be blessed. That blessing to all nations is fulfilled in the new covenant — the covenant sealed in the blood of Christ. "And almost all things are by the law purged with blood; and without shedding of blood is no remission" (Hebrews 9:22). To remit is to pay the cost. Jesus paid the price of our salvation and established a new covenant — not with one nation, but with all who will come to God through His blood.

2. Defining the Symbolism

Of all the elements included in the Jewish Passover, Jesus chose the two most central ones as symbols of His new covenant: the bread and the wine. The final cup of the Passover observance was called the "cup of blessing." Paul the Apostle wrote: "The cup of blessing which we bless, is it not the communion of the blood of Christ? The bread which we break, is it not the communion of the body of Christ?" (1 Corinthians 10:16). The Early Church understood well the significance of these two emblems. They were able to understand better than did the disciples in the Upper Room, for those disciples had not experienced Calvary. They had not yet stood at the foot of the cross to see His sacred blood flowing to the ground and the wounds in His body which would be for the healing of the nations. Only after Calvary would the full impact of the communion observance be understood.

C. Observing the Lord's Supper

1. Frequency

Jesus did not specify a particular frequency for observance of the Lord's Supper. This was left to the believer. This is implied in the words of Jesus to Paul, "as oft as ye drink it" (1 Corinthians 11:25). How often was a matter of choice. The Jewish Passover was once a year. There are evidences that some of the local congregations in the Early Church took communion on a weekly basis. Perhaps the best practice is to take it often enough to keep the memory of our Lord's death before us, and not so frequently as to lose its significance. Many churches observe it monthly and some on a weekly basis. The Bible leaves the frequency to the church.

2. Meanings
   a. Catholic View

The Roman Catholic Church has developed a doctrinal position relative to the sacrament of the Communion which states essentially that the wine literally becomes divine blood and the broken bread, literally the body of Christ. This doctrine is called "transubstantiation," meaning that the elements miraculously change character when consecrated by a priest. A literal interpretation of Jesus' words, "this is my body" would appear to support that view, but we have abundant proof in the Bible that Jesus used metaphor in speaking of Himself. He called Himself a "door" but no one misunderstood that He was becoming a literal door. This and other references are consistent with the message which Jesus gave to Paul, that the purpose of the Sacrament was to keep Christ and His death in our memory.

   b. Luther's View

Martin Luther, father of the Protestant Reformation, would not accept the Roman Catholic view, but wanted to stay as near to it as he could without serious error. He felt that it was wise to move slowly in changing the doctrinal beliefs. To accommodate this, he developed a view of the communion which is called "consubstantiation." This means that the Lord's presence is in the elements, but they do not literally become His body and blood. He used iron to demonstrate his concept. When iron is in the fire it is still iron but the fire is also in the iron and it changes color but not substance.

c. What the Bible Teaches

The purpose of the Lord's Supper is to bring the believer into close communion with the Lord through remembrance of His sacrificial death and identity with that death. We might remember also that there is a close connection with the broken body of Christ and His healing of our own bodies. We are healed through His stripes and communion is an excellent time to apply His promises to our own physical needs.

Another important aspect of the Lord's Supper is found in the words of Christ that He would not drink again of the wine with His followers until "that day when I drink it new with you in my Father's kingdom." This appears to refer to the Marriage Supper which we will share with our Lord after the rapture of the Church (Revelation 19:9).

3. Dangers of Misuse

The Apostle Paul points out some very real dangers in approaching the Lord's Supper unworthily (1 Corinthians 11:27-32). Because the Corinthian church had been careless in communion, taking the Lord's Supper while sin and uncleanness was present in the lives of the participants, sickness and even death resulted. Every communion service should be marked by a deep sense of its meaning. Every believer should approach the Lord's Supper with deep contrition and humility. Within ourselves, none could be counted worthy to partake of that blessed cup and bread. Yet the One who promised that forgiveness awaited our prayer of repentence and promised that we could stand pure before God through the merits of Calvary, enables us to take worthily of those blessed elements.

III. Marriage

Marriage is not always included among the sacraments of the Church; but from antiquity, it has held a position worthy of inclusion, for it is both a sacred ceremony and a divinely ordained function. Our Lord was the source of the Lord's Supper and placed His approval and commands behind Water Baptism, but He also added His blessing to the act of marriage, both by participating in one—making it the scene of His first miracle—and by teaching important lessons related to its sanctity.

A. Historical Origins

1. Its Beginnings

Long before there was any written ritual or established clergy, there was marriage. In fact, God Himself performed the first marriage in Eden as He united Adam and Eve in a holy union, which we call marriage. This union was established because God saw that it was not good for a man to dwell alone. God created Eve from Adam's side and joined them together and the Word declares of that act, "Therefore shall a man leave his father and his mother, and shall cleave unto his wife: and they shall be one flesh" (Genesis 2:24).

Following Adam and Eve's disobedience in the Garden, the second aspect of marriage came into being: the establishment of a family. Now Adam and Eve bore children and were faced with the responsibilities of bringing those children up in ways pleasing to God. The home was established, with all of its relationships and responsibilities.

2. Its Meaning

As the Word declares, marriage is a process or action where two people become "one" in a unity which is intended to parallel the unity between the Heavenly Father and His own Son, Jesus Christ. No matter what the source or type of the ceremony, the Word teaches that the union is made by God. "What therefore God hath joined together, let not man put asunder" (Mark 10:9). Marriage is the holy bond which fulfills the deepest needs of each partner to the marriage and hallows the bearing and rearing of children. It is God's foundation for a stable and happy society.

3. Its Importance

There have always been challenges to the Bible pattern of marriage, but we have seen those challenges grow and become ominous in our day. The secular humanists have sought by a variety of means to cut away the very foundations of the biblical marriage and home. The way for their influence has been paved by lax attitudes toward the sanctity of marriage and the ease with which people can now secure divorces. Added to this is the newer attitude that "consenting adults" have the right to enter into any kind of relationship, regardless of its moral consequences. The same influences are exerting great pressures to lessen the influence of parents on their own children. We must understand the threat which faces the Church and know the Bible foundations for our beliefs.

B. Bible Pattern of Marriage

1. Unity

The ancient form of the family was based on great unity between the family members, growing out of the strength of the union between husband

and wife. The fact that the Word presents marriage as a union whereby the two partners become "one" is instructive. The unity portrayed there is so beautiful and so strong as to reflect the union of the Godhead. However, this unity is not based on a contract alone. It goes deeper than a ceremony. It is based on mutual love and respect.

2. Relationships

The Bible presents an ideal for the family which should be the goal of every family unit. The father is the head of the household, and is to be the spiritual leader of the home. In ancient times, he was the "priest" of the family. This leadership does not imply domination, but rather loving care and guidance for the family. The wife is to love and respect the husband and make place for his rightful headship. The relationship is to be one of mutual love and respect. The Apostle Paul taught that the love should follow the ideal relationship which Christ has with the Church (Ephesians 5:25). The sexual relationship within the marriage is holy and should be entered with mutual love and understanding (Hebrews 13:4 and 1 Corinthians 7:5). Any sexual relationship outside of marriage is sinful and is a sin against a man's own body, as well as a sin against God. All the rhetoric in the world will not make holy what God condemns as sinful and wrong.

Under the parents, God placed the children. They are taught to obey the parents and to love and respect them. The parents are taught to deal lovingly and firmly with their children, not withholding appropriate punishment when it is needed. The key to a biblical family is love, respect and good communication at all times. The fifth and

sixth chapters of the Ephesian letter furnish sound
Bible foundations for the godly Christian home.

3. Sanctity

The Bible places one point of emphasis on the
subject of marriage—it is a union performed by
God. It matters not that the ceremony is formal-
ized by secular persons so far as God is concerned.
The union is a sacred one in His eyes, and is not to
be taken lightly or dissolved with impunity.

C. Divorce

1. Old Testament Practice

Before the time of Moses, there is no mention in
the Bible of any marriages being dissolved. Because of some very real problems among the Israelites and because they did not choose to seek
God's perfect will, the Lord allowed divorce to
dissolve marriages. Through the centuries, the
grounds for such divorces became more and more
lax, and by the time of Christ, it had become a
scandal in their nation. The rights of divorce lay
totally in the hands of the husband—the wife had
no rights. And, a man could divorce his wife for
such slight things as not liking the way she
cooked his meals. The act of divorcement was
also very simple and could be done with very little
effort on the man's part, leaving the wives with
some genuine reasons for despair. It should be
noted that there is little biblical foundation for
what has become both a legal and ecclesiastical
practice—annulment.

2. New Testament Teachings

Jesus laid out the first teachings related to the
strong bond which marriage represented and He
stressed that the one valid grounds for divorce lay
in marital infidelity — adultery. Why is this? The

act of marriage sanctifies the sexual act and is a contract of monogamy — a pledge to be faithful to the companion and the companion alone. The act of adultery is a breach of that contract and stands as the one acceptable basis for divorce taught by our Lord.

Does this mean that there are no other grounds for divorce which may be acceptable in God's sight? Bible scholars consider that the Apostle Paul offers some additional insights in the seventh chapter of 1 Corinthians. There he says: "Art thou bound unto a wife? seek not to be loosed. Art thou loosed from a wife? seek not a wife. But and if thou marry, thou hast not sinned; and if a virgin marry, she hath not sinned. Nevertheless, such shall have trouble in the flesh" (verses 27,28). Divorce is discouraged and the divorcee warned that it isn't "better the second time around." The scars will remain, and so often, children are the greatest victims of our easy divorces.

3. The Church Deals with Divorce

It is a fact of life that many believers are victims of divorces. Many of these divorces happened before the Christian came to Christ. And, not all of the divorces were because the believer was the victim of unfaithfulness on the part of the partner. The following are important considerations for the Church in dealing with this problem:

a. If the divorce was before the believer knew the Lord the divorce and any sins connected with the past should be left in the hands of the Lord who has promised to forgive all sins and cleanse from all unrighteousness.

b. If the divorce is now fact, and the believer realizes that the biblical grounds are questionable, he can only place the matter in the hands of the Lord and make a firm commitment to live a holy, pure life and to be a proper marriage partner in the future.

But what about the rising numbers of Christians who are seeking easy answers to some of the problems of marriage? And does infidelity mean that the believer should then seek a divorce? One Bible truth which has often been ignored is the instruction to forgive one another. This is not always easy but it is Christ-like. The first responsibility of any Christian is to forgive and restore.

Finally, Christians should remember that divorce is not the unforgivable sin. While it is hurtful and disruptive, when it is a fact of life, we should demonstrate Christian love and compassion and make restoration and obedience the goal in our ministry to others.

IV. Errors and Alternative Beliefs

A. Christian Science

Christian Science tends to "spiritualize" away all meaning in the sacraments of the Church. The Lord's Supper is called a "dead rite." And marriage was viewed by Mary Baker Eddy as appropriate only because men had not reached true spiritual maturity.

B. Mormonism

The Mormons teach water baptism for the dead. This is why they place so great an emphasis on genealogies. The Lord's Supper is observed in a way quite different from Christian practice. They partake in pride of their humanity, and sometimes use water instead of wine. As to marriage, the long history of polygamy as practiced until outlawed by state and federal laws is well known. Mormon theology teaches that women can be redeemed only by union with a Mormon man and that by bearing children, they are bearing redeemed, immortal beings.

Questions for Review

1. What act of Jewish religion foreshadows water baptism?
2. What does water baptism mean?
3. Does being baptized in water save us?
4. Why do we use immersion as the only valid method of water baptism?
5. What Jewish Feast is the pattern for our Lord's Supper?
6. What do the bread and wine represent?
7. What does "transubstantiation" mean?
8. Where was marriage instituted?
9. Who performed the first marriage?
10. What single basis for divorce did Jesus allow?

Chapter 10
THE CHURCH

Outline

I. Origins of the Concept
    A. Old Testament Foundations
        1. The Congregation
        2. The Tabernacle/Temple
        3. The Relationships
    B. New Testament Meaning
        1. Called Out

II. Defining the Church
    A. Its Beginning
    B. Ways the Word is Used
        1. A Building
        2. A Congregation
        3. A Universal Fellowship
    C. Relationhip with Christ
        1. His Bride
        2. His Body
        3. A Holy Building

III. Purposes of the Church
    A. Evangelism

    1. Fulfilling the Great Commission
    2. Pattern for Evangelism
    3. Importance of Evangelism
  B. Nurturing the Believers
    1. Teaching
    2. Feeding
    3. Sustaining
    4. Restoring

III. Organization of the Church
  A. Original Structural Patterns
  B. Historical Changes
    1. Effects of Persecution
    2. Growth of Central Power
      a. Political Reasons
      b. Ecclesiastical Considerations
    3. Changes of the Reformation
  C. Function of Organization
    1. Denominational Considerations
    2. Local Churches

IV. The Church at Worship
  A. New Testament Patterns
  B. Origin of Liturgies
  C. Considerations for Our Day
    1. Worshiping the Lord
    2. Proclaiming the Word
    3. Building the Saints
    4. Evangelizing the World

V. Ministry of the Church
  A. Defining the Ministry
    1. Leaders
    2. Servants
  B. The Call
    1. Definition of the Call
    2. Qualification Needed

3. Following the Lord
C. Sanctity of the Calling
   1. Recognizing the Divine Source
   2. Dealing with Failure
VI. Errors and Alternative Beliefs
A. General Cultistic Errors
B. Mormonism
C. Jehovah's Witnesses

I. Origins of the Concept

A. Old Testament Foundations

1. The Congregation

The nearest thing we can find to the New Testament Church in the Old Testament is the name used for Israel: Congregation. While there are significant differences between this Old Testament concept and that of the Church in the New Testament, there are also similarities. The Congregation was a name used for the body of people who were participants with God in the covenant. They had a relationship with God through that covenant and it was so binding a relationship that God accused them of being estranged from Him when they went astray from His Law. God spoke of His relationship with Israel as a marriage and demanded that they be faithful to Him and to His teachings. This union, however, was not so much one of faith as it was of blood lines. Every man or woman born in Israel was considered to be an heir of the covenant.

B. The Tabernacle/Temple

As a vital part of God's relationship with Israel, He ordered the construction of a building, first the

Tabernacle and then the Temple. These buildings were to serve as a center for Israel's worship, but not in the same way as our churches of today serve. The Temple was a place of sacrifice. The Israelites gathered outside and all of the rites were performed by the priests. While there were activities there every day, the people only came at stated times or for required purposes. There were no other copies of the Temple in other areas of the nation. The only ones who went in the Temple were the priests dedicated to that purpose. It was not a house of worship but a center for repentance and honor to God. The people brought their tithes and offerings, but were given very few rights of participation in the religious functions of the Temple.

    3. The Relationships

The people of Israel had no rights to approach God directly. They were required to come through the offices of the priests and to approach God through sacrifices. Even the priests were restricted in their access to God. Only the High Priest had the right to go into the Holy of Holies and he went there only once a year. This entire approach of man to God and God to man was to change with the coming of Christ.

B. New Testament Meaning

    1. Called Out

When God first sought to establish a covenant with men, He began by calling Abram out of Ur of Chaldees. When God was ready to make a nation of Israel in fulfillment of His promises to Abraham, He called them out of Egypt. Egypt was a type of sin. Thus when Christ established the body of believers which were to become the Church, it is not surprising that the root meaning of "church" is the "called out ones." And just as God called Israel to come out of Egypt, so does He call us to "come out from among them, and be ye separate, saith the Lord, and touch not the unclean thing; and I will receive you" (2 Corinthians 6:17).

II. Defining the Church

A. Its Beginning

There are two views related to just when the Church began. Some feel that it started with the beginning of Christ's ministry and that the calling of the twelve disciples marked the introduction of the first ministry. However, the prevailing view is that the Day of Pentecost was the birthday of the Church. This is a valid viewpoint inasmuch as there could truly be no body of believers born through Jesus' blood until that blood was shed. Further, Jesus stressed to His followers that they were not to begin the fulfillment of the Great Commission until they had been "endued with power from on high." The Pentecostal experience is what empowerd those early leaders to witness with authority and effectiveness.

B. Ways the Word is Used

In order to understand a study of the Church, we need to identify ways in which the word is used. The following three meanings are commonly used in our day with the same word to describe them:

1. A Building

It is not uncommon for us to say, "I'm going to the church" when we are going to the church building. We have so identified the church building with the existence of the local church that we confuse meanings if we are not careful. Buildings are important to the purposes of the Church but they are not truly the same.

2. A Congregation

When we speak of our local congregation of believers as the "church," we are nearer to the Bible meaning of the word. We find a similar usage of the word in Romans 16:5 and 1 Corinthians 16:19, where the local "house church" is called the church. So long as we understand that the local congregation is a part of the larger body of believers called the Church, we will avoid diluting the name.

3. A Universal Fellowship

The truest meaning of the Church is as a universal fellowship of believers. This Church is sometimes referred to as the "Church invisible," demonstrating that its boundaries are not defined by denominational names or geographical limits. This Church is comprised of every blood-bought child of God and only the Lord knows truly who is in that wonderful body. We may be assured that there are no hypocrites in that body.

C. Relationship with Christ

The Church is a unique body. It was bought with the terrible price of the blood of Jesus Christ (Ephesians 5:25). He purchased the Church because He loved it. The Word teaches that this relationship between Christ and His Church is a close one, indeed.

1. His Bride

In 2 Corinthians 11:2 and Ephesians 5:25-27 we see the Church pictured as the bride of Christ. We see this relationship defined further in the book of Revelation (19:7; 22:17). Jesus likened

Himself to the Bridegroom and the consummation of the relationship is pictured in Revelation 21:2.

2. His Body

The Apostle Paul also used the word-picture of the human body to show how close is the relationship between Christ and the Church. He is shown as the "head" and the Church as His body (Ephesians 4:16 and Colossians 1:18).

3. A Holy Building

The letter to the Ephesians deals substantially with the Church and one of the illustrations shown there is of a building (2:20-22). The foundation is portrayed there as the prophets and apostles, and Jesus is the Cornerstone. All of these illustrations demonstrate the close relationship between Christ and His Church.

III. Purposes of the Church

While there are social aspects to the Christian Church, it cannot be said that the purpose of the Church is social. Our calling and commission is much higher than that. One measure of the Church's purpose is to represent Christ to the world. We are told that we are ambassadors for Him, a role of interpreting the will and message of our Lord to our generation.

A. Evangelism

1. Fulfilling the Great Commission

It is generally agreed that when a person knows that he is speaking the last words on this earth, the words spoken will reflect the deepest longings and intents of the heart. Our Lord, in the closing days of His ministry here on earth, spoke over and over of the need to reach lost men with the good news of the gospel. The basic commission to fulfill His mission was spoken on three different occasions, and each event added an important dimension to His will.

In Matthew 28:19,20 we are told to go and teach all nations. In Mark 16:15 we are told to go into all the world and preach the gospel to every creature. In Acts 1:8, we are told that we will be witnesses for Christ. Every word on these occasions relates to the responsibility of the Church to witness to the unsaved and to lead men to Christ and His love. This is the highest responsibility of the Church.

2. Pattern for Evangelism

In the first chapter of Acts, the Lord gives the Early Church a pattern for evangelism. They were to begin at Jerusalem, then to go into Judea, then into Samaria, and thence into the uttermost parts of the earth. The disciples did evangelize Jerusalem and some ministry reached into their own province of Judea, but it was not until great persecution scattered the Church that they went everywhere, preaching the Word. Once the message began to move outward, it did not stop until it reached all of the known world and their evangelism was so effective that within the lifetime of the Apostles, it is estimated that ten percent of the people were saved.

While it is necessary to have a strong home front in order to build effective missionary ministries, it is tragic that so many churches have little or no vision for evangelizing beyond their own communities. The Church cannot truly fulfill Christ's plan without a deep involvement with evangelizing the entire earth. This is our highest calling and our greatest challenge.

3. Importance of Evangelism

Long before the disciples were completely prepared, they were sent forth to minister and to preach the good news of the coming Kingdom. It has been demonstrated that the growth of a local church is in direct proportion to the percentage of their resources, both human and monetary, that are committed to soul-winning. God's greatest blessings will never rest on the church that is not deeply committed to doing what the Lord has asked that we do.

B. Nurturing the Believers

1. Teaching

In the listing of ministries in Ephesians 4:11, we see that of teaching. Jesus told us that we are to go and teach. Timothy was instructed to "study" to show himself approved unto God, a workman who need not be ashamed (2 Timothy 2:15). Israel was instructed to make teaching central to the rearing of their families. There were some periods in history where the Church let down in the ministry of teaching and in every instance, the failure was followed by apostasy. It is a fact of history that great revivals often follow intense interest in studying the Word of God. Teaching is a most important ministry of the church for building strong Christians.

2. Feeding

The three-fold purposes of ministry in Ephesians 4:12 are: 1) Perfecting; 2) Ministering; and, 3) Edifying. Paul talks of the importance of spiritual diets, telling the Corinthians that milk represents the "baby food" and meat the diet for the spiritually mature. The Church should keep a balanced spiritual diet on the "table" so that all believers are spiritually nourished.

3. Sustaining

Just as a child requires continuing love, feeding and help to grow into a mature individual, so does the believer need spiritual undergirding for life. When we go through discouragement, our brothers and sisters should offer the needed encouragement. When we hurt, they should be there to pray for us. The Word teaches that we should honor one another, love one another, forgive one another, pray one for another, comfort one another and serve one another. The fellowship of the believers is a brotherhood and it binds us in a family which is wonderful, indeed.

4. Restoring

The Corinthian church had problems. Along with other problems, they had people in the church who were not living the Christian life. Sin was evident and the Apostle Paul encouraged them to deal with this sin, lest it become a cancer in their midst. They did so, but handled it with such love that the sinner was restored to fellowship with God and with the body. Paul said to the Galatians: "Brethren, if a man be overtaken in a fault, ye which are spiritual, restore such an one in the spirit of meekness; considering thyself, lest thou also be tempted. Bear ye one another's burdens, and so fulfill the law of Christ" (6:1,2). The willingness to restore a fallen brother is equated with spirituality.

III. Organization of the Church

A. Original Structural Patterns

When the Church began to grow so rapidly following Peter's Pentecost sermon, it would appear that there was little structure underlying the new entity. In fact, the structure depended on the organization which the Lord had instituted until the growth reached the place that the twelve leaders could no longer cope and they expanded the structure to include helpers. The Church had no buildings and the worship patterns were slowly established to meet the needs of the growing body. Meetings were held in homes and much of the pattern of worship was drawn from the Jewish synagogue services with which the disciples were familiar. Music was in the form of the Jewish chant and the singing was primarily the use of the Psalms, in chant form. The only Bible they had was the Greek Septuagint version of the Old Testament.

With time, the believers adopted the apostolic writings as the New Testament and the growing Church began to adopt worship patterns distinctive to Christianity. After the persecutions abated, they began to build buildings. Changes in society and circumstances brought evolving worship patterns through the years as the Church adapted the elements of worship to meet people's needs.

B. Historical Changes

1. Effects of Persecution

Because of the persecution in the Church before 313 A.D. the worship patterns were not uniform, for the worshippers found it necessary to adapt to whatever facilities and aids were available. Geographic differences and the difficulty of passing ideas from one body to another also brought some differences. In the New Testament, we see descriptions of forms which are thought to have existed with little change for more than a hundred years. They read from the Old Testament, and when available, from the apostolic writings. They sang or chanted the Psalms and the newer hymns, and then preached or taught the Word. Prayer was made for the sick and communion was taken at differing intervals. An offering was sometimes received for needy Christians. The persecution forced many to worship in caves and catacombs.

2. Growth of Central Power

a. Political Reasons

When Rome removed the persecution of the Church, it was not long before Christianity became the official religion of the Roman Empire and from this, it was a short step to the merging of religious and civil authority.

b. Ecclesiastical Considerations

One other reason for centralization of power was the problem of the heresies. To answer these, the Church found it helpful to have a central form of authority so that heresies could be stopped quickly. This brought the episcopal (bishop) form of government with an authoritative head of the Church who ruled through appointed leaders called bishops (and/or presbyters). This did help to stop heresies, but it also placed great power in the hands of the Church leaders.

3. Changes of the Reformation

With the success of Martin Luther and other reformers, there arose a vital interest in lessening the power of the central authority of a leader. With John Calvin and others of similar persuasion, congregational authority was emphasized and the episcopal forms of government began to lose some of their appeal. Of course, not all Protestant movements adopted a form of congregationalism but that part of the movement has generally been the most vital and evangelistic.

C. Function of Organization

Because of the abuses of authority, some have sought to move completely away from any form of a central authority. However, we should also consider what the Bible teaches about being subject to authority and of the need for organization to carry forth the Lord's work efficiently.

1. Denominational Considerations

It is helpful to study church history and see just what has happened to the revival movements through the ages. You will find that every such movement has either been through the structured Church or has become a part of it. Other movements which have failed to become a part of the visible Church have been lost. There are valid reasons for churches and church leaders to bind themselves together in associations or movements in order to better accomplish the vision which God has given them. While there have been some attempts to give specialized meaning to the word "denomination," we are safer using the true meaning, which is simply "the name by which you are known." Within such an association, churches may accomplish more by being part of a larger whole.

World missions and literature publication are two areas where associational relationships are helpful. It is also a help to local churches to have some form of "certification" or licensing of a minister whom they are considering. "And we beseech you, brethren, to know them which labour among you, and are over you in the Lord, and admonish you" (1 Thessalonians 5:12). This is a beneficial service of a church fellowship or denomination.

2. Local Churches

With the episcopal form of government, pastors are appointed by the organization's leaders. With the congregational form of government, the choice for spiritual leader is under the local congregation, using such safeguards as are appropriate. The local church is a part of the larger body of Christ, which we call the Church. There is a growing and Christ-like trend toward a greater sense of respect and appreciation for churches of differing fellowships.

Some have thought the multiplicity of denominations as a weakness. It is possible, also, to see them as offering great diversity and great vitality to the Church. The greatest dangers are in a narrow and selfish view of our own role as a local body of believers. We need to know who the enemy is. We need to recognize the great potential of the Church through the unity for which our Lord prayed (John 17:21). This need not be unity through assimilation of the smaller by the larger, but might well be the unity of love and mutual respect.

IV. The Church at Worship

A. New Testament Patterns

Some have sought to recapture the New Testament patterns of worship for churches of our day. This is not practical and may not even be possible. The New Testament Church had no hymnals and

209

no music as we know it. They had no printed New Testaments, and the earlier Church had no New Testament at all. They had no church buildings and no printed matter. It was a different world. The forms of worship used were those appropriate to their time and their culture. The Holy Spirit has guided the Church in each age to the methods which best communicate the Gospel.

B. Origin of Liturgies

Churches who are involved in modern patterns of worship sometimes reject liturgies and rituals as being meaningless and archaic. We should remember, however, that every ritual grew out of a situation where it was the best answer to a need. The problem is that we often keep a ritual long after it has fulfilled its purpose. Ritual is not inappropriate to the Church, but it should be used with purpose and because it meets the need of the body of believers. Some of the older rituals were devices to teach the Word to people who could not read. Others used repetition to burn vital truths into the hearts of the believers. All churches use them in a greater or a lesser degree.

C. Considerations for Our Day

The purpose of any activity within the Church is to fulfill our Lord's instructions and to accomplish the goals of the Word. For some, there is considerable reaction against any change. For others, change is so attractive that they will change worship patterns with no reason except change.

1. Worshiping the Lord

One purpose of any service in the Church is to worship and praise the Lord. The Early Church gave such worship a principal place in their plans and it is still one of the primary considerations for any service. Such worship should not be simply mechanical, but should be from the hearts of the people.

2. Proclaiming the Word

One of the historic parts of Christian worship has been the preaching of the Word of God. Nothing can take the place of this. Paul reminds us that it is through the "foolishness of preaching" that God will save them that believe (1 Corinthians 1:21). The style and methods of preaching have changed over the centuries, but its purpose remains the same. It is God's tool to reach man through his emotions. Teaching is the way God reaches hearts through the intellect. Both can be effective tools of proclaiming the Word of God.

3. Building the Saints

"Perfecting the saints" is one of Paul's designated functions of the ministry (Ephesians 4:12). He also said that "edifying" was a responsibility of the ministry. If a mother gave birth to a baby, then when the baby was brought home from the hospital set the baby aside to fend for itself, we would doubt her sanity. Yet do we not do the same thing with babes born into the kingdom of God? The discipling of believers is a ministry of high priority to the Church.

4. Evangelizing the World

When the Lord asked us to go into all the world and preach the gospel to every creature, He intended that such evangelization take place. And, it is the responsibility of every believer within the Church to see that this does happen. Such is the work of evangelization, beginning at home and reaching out until we have reached into the most remote areas of the globe. It is important that we witness to our neighbors, but it is also important that the Church fund and operate world missions.

V. Ministry of the Church

A. Defining the Ministry

Paul gives us some definitions of ministries in Ephesians. His list is: Apostles, prophets, evangelists, pastors and teachers. In fact, this is a summary of the ministries as they existed in the Early Church. We use different names in some instances, but there are differing types of ministry used in and for the benefit of the Church in our day. These include pastors, evangelists, missionaries and teachers. But it also includes those who work in such specialized ministries as administration and music. Each can be a holy and God-ordained vocation under the Holy Spirit.

1. Leaders

Ministers are called to be leaders, but leaders in a different sense than that used by the world. Jesus taught that the way up is down. The road to exaltation is through humiliation. We take the lower seat, and honor our brother before ourselves. So the leader must understand that he is a leader in a limited sense of the word. First, the leader is under Christ, and he is totally accountable to the Lord for his leadership. There is authority in the Church, but it is benevolent and loving authority. Those called by the Lord must learn the skills of leadership so that others will follow them willingly and with benefit.

2. Servants

The minister is also called to be a servant, serving the people, but answering to Christ. Ministers are "under-shepherds," working under the Chief Shepherd, Jesus Christ. Any minister should understand the role of the servant. It is only as the leader serves others that he can most truly serve the Lord. Jesus taught us many lessons of servant-hood. When He washed the disciples feet, it was to demonstrate that there could be no arrogance and pride in leadership in the Kingdom.

B. The Call

Not one of the twelve Disciples came to Jesus and asked to be His disciple. They were called. They were chosen. So the Lord chooses His servants and the decision to enter the ministry should begin with a divine call. This call can take many forms, but it is definite and unforgettable. Some have wanted to go into the ministry for the wrong reasons and this can lead to heartaches and failure.

1. Definition of the Call

For the Twelve, the call came directly from Jesus Himself. Paul also had such a divine visitation when Christ came to him on the Damascus road and called him to be a minister to the Gentiles. Whatever the form of the call, the one thinking of entering the ministry should wait on the Lord for His will and direction. The trials and responsibilities of the ministry are too great to endure without a deep sense of God's divine will.

2. Qualification Needed

God doesn't always call men because they are qualified for the task He places before them. But

He does call those who are capable of becoming qualified. It is the responsibility of the minister to prayerfully seek ways of studying and preparing for the high calling of God in Christ Jesus. Paul told young Timothy to study. He did not define the curriculum or set limits as to when and how. He simply asked that he begin a process of study and use whatever means could best meet the end of rightly dividing the Word of truth.

3. Following the Lord

It is important that any Church leader learn to follow the Lord. This will mean that the ear must be tuned to the Master's voice and that no conditions should be set for obedience. When the Lord calls ministers, He asks for unconditional surrender to His will. And, there are times when the leader finds it necessary to pray "not my will, but thine be done" with our Lord. Our hearts desire a road map. He gives a hand. We want a picture, but He gives us the Holy Spirit as our "walker alongside" and constant Companion.

C. Sanctity of the Calling

God's call is a divine call. When God places His hand on a life, it follows that the Church should respect that call and make place for its fulfillment. David was blessed of the Lord because he knew the danger of putting his hand on God's anointed servant. Saul was not without sin and he had done some things which might have justified a lesser view, but it was not Saul whom David was honoring — it was the God who had called Saul.

2. Dealing with Failure

One of the most puzzling dilemmas faced by the Church is how to deal with failure on the part of a minister. Ministers are human and they are not always as wise as they should be. There are two considerations which are related to this problem. First, we should recognize that with leadership goes great responsibility. "Unto whomsoever much is given, of him shall much be required" said our Lord (Luke 12:48).

The leader who errs is accountable to God for that failure and bears a greater load of responsibility because of the trust placed in him. The second consideration, however, is that the Church is accountable to God for how we treat leaders. We are not asked to condone sin or failure, but we are asked to consider the Lord's call and ask the Lord to deal with the problem. We need not condone wrong to have compassion. We need not be weak to seek restoration and correction. If all is done with genuine love and respect, we can avoid a lot of heartache, and redeem lives which would otherwise be destroyed. We must remember that the Church is God's business.

VI. Errors and Alternative Beliefs

A. General Cultistic Errors

Before we discuss some specific errors related to the Church, we might consider what is a general error of most cults. The cultists virtually always present their own ideas and doctrinal approach as the only valid one. They make little or no place for dissenting beliefs. The appeal of the cults is that they present themselves as the "only truth" to gullible people.

B. Mormonism

The Mormon Church teaches that legitimate Christianity was driven from the earth in the first ten centuries, and that true Christianity was found through Joseph Smith and his spurious scriptures. They view all churches as false and teach that only through Mormonism is there any salvation.

C. Jehovah's Witnesses

Similar to Mormonism, the Jehovah's Witnesses teach that they are the only true messengers of Jehovah God and that salvation can come only through accepting their message. They teach that the Lord has already returned and is cleansing the spiritual temple, getting ready for the 144,000 who alone will be the faithful. The Witnesses see themselves as God's messegers to bring the world into the righteous millennium.

Questions for Review

1. What is the nearest equivalent to the Church in Judaism?
2. What was the birthday of the Church?
3. What three "word-pictures" does to Bible use to show Christ's relationship to the Church?
4. What are the two primary areas of ministry for the Church?
5. Why is evangelism important to the Church?
6. Why did the Early Church move toward strong central government?
7. Why is praise important to the Church?
8. What is the primary role of church denominations?
9. Why should a minister have a divine call?
10. What is the view of virtually all cults toward the Church?

Chapter 11

THE UNSEEN WORLD

Outline

I. Origin of Angels
  A. Their Beginnings
    1. Angelic Order
    2. Relationship to the Creator
  B. Their Function
    1. To Worship God
    2. To Serve God

II. Lucifer's Rebellion
  A. Lucifer's Role
  B. Lucifer's Sin
  C. Lucifer's Fall
  D. Lucifer's Followers
  E. Satan's Kingdom
  F. Satan's Work
    1. The Tempter
    2. The Hinderer

    3. The Accuser
    4. The Liar
III. Demons
    A. Agents of Satan
       1. Doing Satan's Work
       2. Enemies of Redemption
    B. Demons and Men
       1. Possession
       2. Oppression
    C. Limits of Demonic Authority
       1. Limits Set by God
       2. Limits Set by Saints
    D. Demons and the Believer
       1. Keeping our Lives Free
       2. Bringing Deliverance to Others
IV. Angels
    A. Their Role
       1. Messengers of God
       2. Protectors of the Believer
       3. The Worship of God
       4. Concern for Sinners
    B. Angels in Eternity
V. Errors and Alternative Beliefs
    A. Satanism
    B. Spiritism
    C. Modernism

I. Origin of Angels

If we believe the Bible to be the Word of God, we must accept the truth that angels exist, and that they are involved in the affairs of men. From Genesis to Revelation we find records of their existence and activities. Jesus taught that they were real, and the Apostles acknowledged their existence and work. Our belief in their existence need not be based on any personal proofs, for God's Word consistently affirms their role in the plan of God.

A. Their Beginnings

The Bible is silent as to when angels were created, but we do know from the Bible that "By him were all things created, that are in heaven, and that are in earth, visible and invisible, whether they be thrones, or dominions, or principalities, or powers; all things were created by him, and for him" (Colossians 1:16). We also know that their creation predates man's own origins.

There are no Bible references to the angels calling God their "Father." They do not belong to the family of God, nor are they heirs of God's redemption. The angels do not have the privilege of being born again and of being an heir to the promise of God through Christ Jesus.

1. Angelic Order

Everything created by God is orderly. The heavens have a magnificent order and all of creation on earth follows a consistent order. God is not the author of confusion and disorder. He created the angels with an order and a basic organizational structure. We are not given many details as to what that order means but we are told of its existence.

The highest in the order of angels is the Archangel. Even though there are Apocryphal references to seven archangels the Bible only gives that title to one: Michael. Gabriel seems to have been a highly-placed messenger for the Lord, carrying vital information to Daniel and to Mary, mother of our Lord. The name "Michael" means "who is like unto the Lord." "Gabriel" means "God's hero." The angelic order to which Gabriel belongs is not named.

There are two other orders of angels in the Bible: cherubim and seraphim. The Seraphim are mentioned only in the vision of Isaiah 6 and their function appears to be the praise and worship of God. The cherubim, however, appear in numerous Bible references beginning with the fact that one of this order of angels was charged with the duty of keeping men from the Garden of Eden after the fall. When God gave instructions for the building of the Tabernacle, He included the fact that the cherubim were to be used in the design of the tapestries and engravings of the cherubim were to be over the Ark of the Covenant on the Mercy Seat. God pictures Himself as dwelling "between the cherubims" (1 Samuel 4:4).

Other mention of angels include "angels of the nations" (Daniel 10) and "elect angels" (1 Timothy 5:21). These do not appear to be names for angelic orders, but descriptions of their duties and functions and the fact that some elected to remain true to God during Lucifer's rebellion.

2. Relationship to the Creator

As mentioned earlier, angels do not have the privilege of being sons of God or of being counted among the redeemed. They do, however, have a special relationship close to the Creator. They dwell close enough to God to face Him (Matthew 18:10). They always work in complete harmony and obedience with the Heavenly Father, and carry out His will with all honesty and diligence.

B. Their Function

1. To Worship God

Throughout the Word of God, we find abundant references to the fact that the angels worship and praise God. In the sixth chapter of Isaiah, we find one of the most memorable descriptions of angels in this role. The book of Revelation also demonstrates the fact that their praises have been continuous and substantial. The seraphim, in particular, are assigned this holy duty, but all angels participate in God's praise.

2. To Serve God

Angels are God's messengers carrying His words to men. Daniel was the recipient of angelic messages, as were other of the prophets of Old Testament. Mary and Joseph received messages delivered by the angels. Abraham talked with angels and received messages from their lips. However, they are more than "heavenly messenger boys." Angels also carry out certain acts of judgment at God's request, as we witness in the destruction of Sodom and Gomorrah. They have been used in battles and have served to turn dangers aside from servants of the Lord.

II. Lucifer's Rebellion

A. Lucifer's Role

The Bible does not give us a total picture of Lucifer's plot and fall, but we are given a number of intimations from which we may draw some fairly clear and consistent observations. We do know that Lucifer was the angel of light and was in an exalted postition, perhaps being an Archangel. He was beautiful and was entrusted with a great deal of authority among the heavenly beings. The exalted position to which he had been entrusted proved to be his downfall.

B. Lucifer's Sin

No matter how we analyze Lucifer's sin, we find that egotism is at the heart of it all. Isaiah records the scene for us: "How art thou fallen from heaven, O Lucifer, son of the morning! how art thou cut down to the ground which didst weaken the nations! For thou hast said in thine heart, I will ascend into heaven, I will exalt my throne above the stars of God: I will sit also upon the mount of the congregation, in the sides of the north: I will ascend above the heights of the clouds; I will be like the most High" (Isaiah 14:12-14). Five times the personal pronoun demonstrates the pride and covetousness which marked his downfall. As always, his sin began in his heart and attitudes and worked outward to his actions.

C. Lucifer's Fall

Jesus said, "I beheld Satan as lightning fall from heaven" (Luke 10:18). There was no way God could allow rebellion to go unpunished. When Lucifer placed his own will above God's will, he crossed over into the state of sinfulness and lost all rights to the holy estate to which God had appointed him. He became Satan, the deceiver, and was cast out of heaven. At that point, there began a warfare which has raged since that time. Satan declared war against God and his attempts to ascend to the heights of authority and power have never ended.

D. Lucifer's Followers

The Word teaches us that a significant number of angels sided with Lucifer and because of that, were cast out of heaven with him. There are intimations in Revelation 12 that one-third of the angels might have been included in this rebellion. Such interpretation is based on interpreting the "stars" there as the sinning angels and the events recorded there as pointing to the ages before Adam and Eve. Most certainly, there were a significant number of the angels who fell from their first estate (Jude 6). Jude tells us that these fallen angels are "reserved in everlasting chains" and are kept in everlasting chains until the day of judgment. Some have thought demons to be these fallen angels but the Bible does not give us sufficient insight to make that claim and the Jude reference would tend to support the idea that demons are another type of unholy entity working with Satan to accomplish his ungodly works.

E. Satan's Kingdom

Lucifer, the fallen angel of light, became Satan, the deceiver. His kingdom is of this world. He is the prince of the powers of the air (Ephesians 2:2). He is called the "god of this world" (2 Corinthians 4:4). He held the power of the kingdom of death until Christ's, in His own death, took control of the power of death over the redeemed. Satan yet has control of the kingdom of death for unregenerate man.

F. Satan's Work

1. The Tempter

From the moment that Satan came to Eve in the Garden of Eden, he has carried forth his schemes through temptation. There are three avenues whereby we are tempted: 1) Our flesh, 2) The world and 3) Satan. Many of our temptations come because of things which appeal to our fleshly desires. Other temptations come because of the influences of the world and worldly people around us. But, even as Jesus was tempted of Satan, so are we tempted to sin by the master of temptation— our adversary, the devil.

2. The Hinderer

Paul wrote to the church at Thessalonica, "We would have come unto you, even I Paul, once and again; but Satan hindered us" (1 Thessalonians 2:18). Satan hinders the work of God whenever he can. He delayed the messenger of God trying to reach Daniel (Daniel 10:13). Satan loves to throw roadblocks in the way of God's people and to disrupt, when he can, the work of evangelism.

3. The Accuser

In the opening verses of Job, we find a scene where God is confronted by Satan. God spoke of Job's faithfulness but Satan accused Job of being obedient and faithful because of God's goodness to him. The tests which Job went through were brought on by Satan's accusations. In Revelation 12:10, he is called "the accuser of our brethren."

4. The Liar

Jesus taught us that Satan is a liar and the father of lies. He used deception to trick Eve into sinning. He uses lies and deceptions to draw men away from godly influences. He paints sin as alluring and the results of sin as beneficial. Not only is he a liar, but he also has lying spirits who do his work in the world.

We should know that the common image people have of the devil is not accurate. This image grew out of the drama of the middle ages, when the church sought to teach Bible lessons by way of plays. People always enjoy comedy, but they could not give funny lines or characterization to Jesus or to other Bible characters except the devil. For this reason, they created the image of the sly character with horns and a tail, dressed in red, who was the "fall guy" and furnished the comedy which the people enjoyed. And Satan doubtlessly enjoys this characterization which casts him in the role of a blundering, malevolent but lovable guy. He is attractive and his personal beauty still makes him deceptive to many. In the ancient drama, the writers gave the devil the best lines, but they also distorted the picture of this one who goes about as a roaring lion, seeking whom he may devour.

Our best defense against Satan is knowledge of his tactics. Paul has said, "Lest Satan should get an advantage of us: for we are not ignorant of his devices" (2 Corinthians 2:11). A knowledge of the Word of God is vital to our spiritual defenses. And a study of the ways in which Satan accomplishes his purposes will arm us against his attacks. Paul tells us of the armor which is so vital in turning aside his fiery darts (Ephesians 6:11-17).

III. Demons

A. Agents of Satan

The Bible offers no concrete evidences as to where demons come from. As pointed out earlier, it is questionable that they are the fallen angels, for these are spoken of as being in chains. Whatever their source, they are spirits from Satan and hold a significant place in the war for the souls of men.

1. Doing Satan's Work

Satan is the father of demons and they do his bidding. We do know that they exist in large numbers, considering the "legion" of demons that inhabited the demoniac of Gadara. Satan is skilled at imitating the works of God with a hellish twist. In demonic activity, we can see a perversion of the work of the Holy Spirit, for these unholy spirits can and do come into the willing vessels, controlling and using them.

2. Enemies of Redemption

Demons are particularly adept at frustrating God's plan for the lives of people who allow themselves to become open to demonic influences. The Bible talks of lying spirits (1 Kings 22:22), seducing spirits (1 Timothy 4:1), familiar spirits (Leviticus 20:27) and unclean spirits (Mark 1:27). These are only representative texts, for there are many references to both familiar spirits and unclean spirits. Those who have come out of the error of Spiritism say that the messages received in the seances are from demonic powers and that the person getting the message is called "the familiar." The fact that these messages frequently tell facts about a dead person which could not be known to the medium is because the "familiar spirits" know intimate details of the lives of the dead. They may also account for the rising popularity of "psychics" and their professed ability to reveal secrets of the lives of the gullible people who are drawn to them.

The rise of interest in the world of occult knowledge is bringing more and more demon possession in our society. Demons always despise the blood of Christ and have been known to react violently in seances when the blood is mentioned. Satan hates Calvary and all truths related to Christ's death for the salvation of mankind. It was at Calvary that Satan received his worst defeat and demons work very hard to hide the truth of the cross from mankind.

B. Demons and Men

Demons find their reason for existence in their relationship to men. When the demons who inhabited the body of the demoniac of Gadara were confronted by Christ, they asked that they be allowed to go into another body and He cast them into swine.

1. Possession

There are many references in the Word of God to demon possession. We find that the manifestations of demonic possession work mostly on the mind and nervous system. We are told that there are many people in the insane institutions of our day for which there is no evidence of any physical ailment. Psychiatry has tried to find answers, but their work has been one of the most notable failures related to health. Psychiatry has no answers for demon possession. Psychology cannot explain nor suggest workable answers for these victims of Satan's plot. Science may laugh at the Bible references to demon possession, but our Lord knew the terrible truth of this curse to men and used His power to deliver people from such affliction.

Demonic possession results from a heart open to Satan's influence. Many hearts and lives are opened to this by their obsession with occult knowledge. Books are sold by the million encouraging people to dabble in the black arts. The rise of witchcraft has brought countless people under the influence of demon powers. Rock music has been a strong influence on young people to turn them to demonic activities. The high rate of suicide among youths attests to the force of demonic activity in our day. Many games which appear innocent are actually tools of Satan to entrap young people in the occult world.

 2. Oppression

Another form of Satan's attack against people is by demonic oppression. This is influence from without. It is not control of the life, but powerful influence to alter the life. Oppression can be very hurtful and can cause grave consequences, but it is not the same as possession, whereby demons invade the body and control the life. The Apostle Paul's "thorn in the flesh" may be viewed as an example of this type of activity.

 C. Limits of Demonic Authority

 1. Limits Set by God

Demons have power, but they are not all-powerful. They must operate within the limits set by God. They cannot read minds. They are not privy to God's plan for our lives. They can hear our words, it would seem, and thus can act on any discouragement or doubts we may voice. They are allowed to afflict people who are open and receptive to their attacks, but cannot go where they are resisted and unwelcomed.

2. Limits Set by Saints

There is no Bible basis for the belief that Christians can be possessed of demons and still remain a Christian. Jesus told of the life that had been cleansed, but not inhabited. The unclean spirit who had been forced out of that life came and found the life unfilled and bringing seven other demons worse than himself, took up his abode there (Matthew 12:43-45). If we are filled with the Spirit of God, we will not be in danger of any demonic possession. "Ye cannot drink the cup of the Lord and the cup of devils: ye cannot be partakers of the Lord's table, and of the table of devils" (1 Corinthians 10:21). Pure water will not flow out of an unclean heart nor filthy water from a pure heart. Possession constitutes control. No man can serve two masters. While the messengers of Satan can buffet and test the child of God, he has no power to enter and control the life dominated by Christ and filled with the Holy Spirit.

D. Demons and the Believer

1. Keeping our Lives Free

We can make the devil flee by resisting him. We can prevent demonic control by being filled with the Spirit. An old proverb says that an idle mind is the devil's playground. If we are preoccupied with selfish ends or desires, we make ourselves vulnerable to Satan's attack. The protection of the believer lies in the Spirit-controlled life. If we study the Bible as we should, we will learn the lessons which will keep us from sin. If we pray as we should, we will bring the Spirit's aid in shielding us from the wiles of the enemy. If we fortify our lives with spiritual armor, we can withstand the attack of Satan. The battle for our souls is spiritual and our armor is spiritual. God has furnished us every protection we need to keep our lives victorious in Christ.

2. Bringing Deliverance to Others

With the rising influence of demonic activity, there is a growing need for Christians to be filled with the Spirit so that they may pray the prayer of deliverance for those who are possessed of demons. Not every sickness represents demon possession. Not every emotional problem is caused by demon possession. The Church needs discernment to know how to deal with these vile forces. Our prayer for deliverance for the possessed should be based on sound Bible principles. We should approach this in love and understanding as well as in faith and in the power of the Holy Ghost. Many have been embarrassed and driven from the fellowship of the church by mishandling of the subject of demons. They are real and they are a threat to our society, but the Lord can and will give us wisdom and discretion so that we may bring true deliverance without pain and emotional scars.

IV. Angels

A. Their Role

After the fall of the disobedient angels, there remained a mighty host of faithful and obedient servants of God. Their number is so vast that we are only told that they are "an innumerable company" (Luke 2:13). And as the fallen angels and demon powers serve the ends of Satan, so do the angels of Heaven serve the Heavenly

Father and help to advance His plan of redemption.

1. Messengers of God

The angels serve as God's messengers and have done so since the early pages of the Bible. They carried messages to Abraham and delivered God's message to Jacob. They talked with the prophets and brought the good news of Christ's birth to Mary and Joseph. They are invisible agents of God and while they can be seen when it serves God's purposes for this to happen, they belong principally to the unseen world.

2. Protectors of the Believer

Psalm 91 is the beloved Psalm of servicemen. In its message are these words: "For he shall give his angels charge over thee, to keep thee in all thy ways" (verse 11). This is the message which Satan distorted to Jesus in the temptation. He sought to get our Lord to tempt God, but Jesus was too wise to do so. Guardian angels are a reality, but they will not protect us from foolish mistakes. They will keep us from dangers which are not brought on by our own folly. Many times we are made aware of the narrow brushes we have with disaster and see the hand of God working on our behalf. But may there not be many more dangers that we will never know about until we get home?

3. The Worship of God

The book of Revelation shows that the angels continue to praise God and will for all time. This is one of the purposes of their creation and they are faithful to fulfill their duties. The throne room of Heaven is filled with the praises of God. God loves to dwell where His praises are abundant. This is why He comes to dwell among our praises (Psalm 22:3).

4. Concern for Sinners

We are told in Luke 15 of a joy in Heaven over souls which are redeemed. Angels know the penalty of sin. They know the reality of hell. They know the love of Jesus which purchased our salvation. And they know what a marvellous happiness comes to the Heavenly Father when one of those for whom His Son died comes to the cross and accepts Christ as Saviour. It is reason for rejoicing. Angels are concerned in the plan of redemption and care when men are redeemed.

B. Angels in Eternity

In the book of Revelation we find numerous references to the role of angels in the events marking the end of our age and the beginnings of eternity. Angels will serve as God's agents of judgment and will pour out His divine wrath on a world which has rejected His love and redemption. They will be messengers to carry divine messages and they will continue to furnish the beautiful songs of praise which will resound through the courts of Heaven. However, they will be joined by a throng who are redeemed, and who will be given a share in the operation of His Kingdom, for the saints of God will assume a rightful share in singing God's praises and doing His eternal works through the ages.

V. Errors and Alternative Beliefs

A. Satanism

In recent years, we have seen a tremendous rise in the worship of Satan. This religion, which would have seemed unthinkable a few years ago, has grown tremendously because of the influence of music dedicated to the praise of Satan and the advancement of his kingdom. The basic doctrine of these followers is that Satan controls the majority of people and he will continue to grow in power and influence until he overcomes God and will reign in the end. Such, of course, is the ambition of Satan, but we know just how false the idea really is. We have "seen the back of the book" and how the battle really ends.

Witchcraft is also involved with demon powers and Satan worship and they use perversions of Christian practice to defile and pollute what is holy. They use an inverted cross, and quote the Lord's prayer backwards. They are deceiving countless people who want to believe their doctrine of self-gratification and unlimited carnality.

B. Spiritism

Spiritism is a milder form of religion which involves a preoccupation with talking with "the dead" and learning about the future from occult activities. This is the same religion forbidden in the Bible. The reason it is forbidden is its involvement with demons and the frequency with which the participants are possessed by these evil spirits. Any form of occult activity is dangerous, and should be strictly avoided by the child of God.

C. Modernism

Modernism tends to laugh at the idea of Satan. The modernists do not believe that the Bible is to be taken literally and so deny the existence of Satan except as a myth. They use what they like to call a rational approach to the Bible, but their approach elevates the mind of man above the revealed Word of God. Of course, they do not believe in angels for the same reasons. What cannot be comprehended by the five senses is rejected by these practitioners of humanism in its varying forms.

Questions for Review

1. Who is the one angel called an "archangel" in the Bible?
2. In their relationship to God, how do angels differ from men?
3. What was Satan's sin?
4. What single trait best identifies Satan?
5. Why does Satan fight against God's plan of redemption?
6. How is demon possession different from demon oppression?
7. What prevents a Christian from being possessed by demons?
8. What is needed to deliver people from demon possession?
9. How do angels serve the believer today?
10. What is the great danger of studying occult knowledge?

12

SECOND COMING
OF CHRIST

Outline

I. Death
  A. Death of the Believer
    1. Rest
    2. Present With the Lord
    3. Awaiting the Sound of the Trumpet
    4. No Purgatory
  B. Death of the Sinner
    1. Isolation
    2. Torment
    3. Awaiting Final Judgment
II. Christ's Return Promised
  A. Old Testament Prophecies
  B. Christ's Promises
  C. Angelic Confirmation
  D. Apostolic Teachings

III. Nature of Christ's Coming
  A. Unexpected
    1. The Day Unknown
    2. Types Used by Jesus
    3. Israel
    4. Tribulation and the End
      a. Post-Tribulation Teaching
      b. Mid-Tribulation Teaching
      c. Pre-Tribulation Teaching
  B. His Return is Personal
    1. It is Actual
    2. It is Visible
    3. It is Glorious
  C. Rapture of the Saints
    1. Bodily Resurrection
      a. Nature of the Resurrection
      b. Immortal Bodies
    2. The First Resurrection
  D. Marriage Supper of the Lamb

IV. Christ's Return to Earth
  A. The Great Tribulation
  B. The Man of Sin
  C. The Battle of Armageddon
  D. Consummation of the Age
  E. Christ's Reign on Earth
    1. Postmillennialism
    2. Amillennialism
    3. Premillennialism

V. Errors and Alternative Views
  A. Jehovah's Witnesses
  B. Seventh Day Adventists
  C. Spiritism
  D. Liberal Theology

There are few subjects in human experience which create so much interest as does that of what happens to people when life ends. The old adage: "The only things certain in life are death and taxes" sums up man's realization that death is the end of each life. Yet what happens beyond the grave has concerned philosophers and teachers from the earliest times recorded in our writings. All religions deal with the subject in some way. Our purpose is to see what God has revealed about this matter.

I. Death

A. Death of the Believer

There have been many books written and a host of testimonies abound which tell of the experiences of people who have died and then came back to life. Some of these experiences accord quite well with what we know of life after death from the Bible, but others are totally false to the clear message of God's Word. Spiritism has fascinated many people and some, such as Bishop Pike, have sought proofs of life after death by turning to the practitioners of spiritism and their seances. The consistent error of the messages received from these mediums is that all people who die enter a realm of happiness and fulfillment. Such is not sound doctrine, but it appeals to those who are not well grounded in the Word of God.

There are areas of knowledge about life immediately beyond the grave which are not fully understood. We can study the beautiful picture of the coming new heaven and new earth and imagine that the believer who has passed from this life is in that New Jerusalem walking on streets of gold. What does the Bible teach?

1. Rest

"And I heard a voice from heaven saying unto me, Write, Blessed are the dead which die in the Lord from henceforth: Yea, saith the Spirit, that they may rest from their labors; and their works do follow them" (Revelation 14:13). The Christian life is described in the Bible as a battle. The believer, when he has lived a full life, comes to the end of life weary with the struggle and earnestly desiring rest. This is one of the most welcomed of states which we are told awaits the believer after this life has ended. Even in these days of leisure time and frequent vacations there comes a time when rest is the most welcomed of life conditions. For the child of God, death is a time of rest.

2. Present With the Lord

While there are a number of things which we are not told about the state of the believer following death, we do know that he is in the presence of the Lord (2 Corinthians 5:8; Philippians 1:23). Jesus told the story of Lazarus and the rich man. In that story (not called a parable in the text) we see that Lazarus is in the presence of Abraham, which was a way of saying to a Jew that he was in God's very presence.

3. Awaiting the Sound of the Trumpet

The Word teaches that the saints who have died before the return of Christ are awaiting the sounding of the trumpet, at which time their resurrected bodies will be reunited with their spirits and they will enter into the next phase of eternal life.

4. No Purgatory

During the "dark ages," Roman Catholic theology adopted a view that few people were worthy of going directly into the presence of the Lord at the time of death. Thus they developed a teaching that the dead go into a place which they call "purgatory" which would serve for final cleansing for the baptized believer. This teaching had great appeal both for clergy and constituents. For the church members, it appeared that one could live whatever kind of life he wished and short of committing a sin worthy of excommunication, the member could expect to be purged in purgatory and still inherit the promises of Heaven later.

For the clergy, the teaching placed great power and means of financial gain in the hands of the church, for the clergy could be paid to offer prayers which were thought to shorten the time a soul was in purgatory. This doctrine eventually led to another false teaching — that some people who died were so holy that they had excess holiness which was somehow given to the church, and for a price, this could be transferred to the sensual one who had died. This was the basic error which caused Martin Luther's break with Roman Catholicism.

The Bible teaches that our holiness is bound up in the grace of Christ and not in our personal worthiness. There is not one shred of Bible which can be made to confirm the idea of a purgatory. What you are at death will determine once and for all time your eternal destiny.

B. Death of the Sinner

Death is the result of Adam's sin. From the date of that first rebellion against God, man has carried the penalty of physical death. "As in Adam all die" says the Word. While faith in Christ will bring new life to the believer, it does not mean that the penalty of the body has been abolished. Man's appointment with death is sure. For the child of God, this means only that God has moved the believer to a better world and the body alone enters into the process called death. For the sinner, however, death is the beginning of a process of eternal death. All bodies are corruptible, as the Apostle Paul taught us, but the believers will "put on incorruption" after death. For the sinner, this is not a promise.

1. Isolation

The story of Lazarus and the rich man emphasizes the loneliness of the sinner who is separated from God and from all sense of His presence. The sinner in this life seldom appreciates how much he is the beneficiary of God's presence and expressed love. The sinner enjoys many of the blessings which come alike to the saint and the sinner. The presence of the Lord abounds in our world, even for those who are little conscious of His presence. However, at death, the sinner is isolated from God's presence and all effects of His divine love. Doubtlessly, this is one of the greatest punishments to be endured by the sinner after death.

2. Torment

The rich man was in flames and torment. This was not a picture of an age which would come in the future — it was a reality for the sinner after death.

3. Awaiting the Final Judgment

Even as the sinner endures the torments of hell, he awaits a sure day when all men will be called to stand before God and following that great day of judgment, he has hope only of more torment in an eternity apart from God and in perpetual fire.

There have been a number of attempts to soften or explain away the teachings of the Bible regarding the future state of the sinner. Yet all of the references in the Bible which speak of Hell in terms of time use the same words of eternal as are used about Heaven. Punishment for the lost is just as eternal as is Heaven and joy for the righteous.

II. Christ's Return Promised

It is helpful to differentiate between the "Rapture of the Church" and the "Return of Christ to earth." The first speaks of the time when the trump of God will sound and the dead in Christ shall be raised to meet Him in the air. The second speaks of the return of Christ with His saints to overcome the Antichrist and establish His kingdom on earth. The prophecies do not always yield to an easy division between those two distinct events, but we will follow them here for clarity and will apply them to the Word of God following that distinction when possible.

The study of last things is a popular one, but it is also a difficult one for the honest scholar. As we approach this subject, we should be aware that there are wide differences of interpretation between scholars who are sincere and honest in their presentations and who accept the divine source of the Bible. It will be helpful if we remember that prophecy is filled with symbolism and that those symbols are not always as clear as we would wish. Even though there were a multitude of prophecies regarding our Lord's first advent, few Jewish scholars expected Him to come as He did. They simply interpreted the prophecies differently.

What we will present here are applications represented by the mainstream of Evangelical thought in our day. Not all scholars will agree in all particulars and we should have charity toward those who sincerely differ with our interpretations. In the last two centuries, we have seen some major changes in prophetic interpretation. The dispensational approach has grown in acceptance and has become the majority view. It is the view accepted by most Pentecostals and will be followed here.

A. Old Testament Prophecies

Isaiah 61 is the prophecy read by Jesus in the Synagogue (Luke 4:18, 19), but He stopped after the words, "acceptable year of the Lord." Why? Because the balance of that prophecy was related to His second coming. You will also find that the visions of Daniel covered both the first and the second advents of Christ. This was one of the sources of confusion among the Jews and even among the disciples, as they had real difficulty in accepting the fact that Jesus would die on the cross, and that His kingdom would not come until many other events had taken place.

The Old Testament does not specifically foretell the ascension of Jesus and His return in the clouds, but we do have teachings there of events which were not fulfilled in His first coming and which He showed us would happen after an interval of time. Job gives us one of the most compelling forecasts of the future: "I know that my redeemer liveth, and that he shall stand at the latter day upon the earth: and though after my skin worms destroy this body, yet in my flesh shall I see God: Whom I shall see for myself, and mine eyes shall behold, and not another; though my reigns be consumed within me" (Job 19:25-27).

B. Christ's Promises

"I go to prepare a place for you. And if I go and prepare a place for you, I will come again, and receive you unto myself; that where I am, there ye may be also" (John 14:2,3). These are the words of Jesus as He neared the time of the cross. He spoke often about His second coming and gave us details which guide us as we anticipate His return. The disciples were so caught up in the idea that the Lord would establish His kingdom on earth in their day that Jesus had to tell them frequently that He would come again and that the balance of the prophecies related to the Messiah would not be fulfilled until that final day.

C. Angelic Confirmation

Not only did the Old Testament prophets foretell events which would be fulfilled by the second coming of Christ, and our Lord Himself tell us that He would come again, but the angels at the time of His ascension also gave clear promises of His return: "This same Jesus, which is taken up from you into heaven, shall so come in like manner as ye have seen him go into heaven" (Acts 1:11).

D. Apostolic Teachings

The Apostle Peter taught: "The day of the Lord will come as a thief in the night" (2 Peter 3:10). The Apostle John gave us the Revelation, which abounds in teaching related to the return of Christ. And the Apostle Paul gave us a rich storehouse of teachings related to many aspects of the second advent. His

Thessalonian letters were written to correct false teachings related to the second coming and to present the truth about this event to come. The Early Church lived in continual expectation of the imminent return of Jesus. In fact, our Lord taught that believers should always live in that expectation and the early believers did this.

III. Nature of Christ's Coming

A. Unexpected

    1. The Day Unknown

Jesus clearly taught that men would not know the precise time of His coming. "But of that day and hour knoweth no man, no, not the angels of heaven, but my Father only" (Matthew 24:36). As we shall see, Jesus did teach that there would be signs which would foretell the "season" of His coming or which would serve to remind believers that He would return. It is a fact of history that men have seen signs similar to those which our Lord foretold and some of these were so compelling that people expected Him to come momentarily — yet the coming was delayed. This appears to some as an unfair approach, but our Lord taught the importance of expecting and remaining ready for His coming. The hazard to our spiritual survival is the idea expressed by Jesus in Matthew 24: "My lord delayeth his coming" (verse 48). Anticipation of His return helps keep us true to Christ.

Jesus told the parable of the ten virgins to illustrate the importance of watching for His return. The signs of His coming keep us alert and the uncertainty of the hour warn that His coming will be unexpected. The cry of "peace and safety" will be heard when the end draws near and show how little man truly expects the Lord to return here and now.

2. Types Used by Jesus

Jesus used common things to help illustrate the nature of His second coming. Some of these related to weather. He told how the Jews could look at the skies and forecast coming weather, but were little concerned with the signs which would point to the end of the age. He used lightning to illustrate the suddenness of His return. The fig tree was also used to show that physical changes in circumstances would show the season of His return. Each of these demonstrates the fine balance between an awareness of the fact that His coming is imminent and the knowledge that we can never safely assume that His coming is delayed.

3. Israel

Apart from the things used by Jesus to illustrate the season of His return, we have the powerful illustration of the Jewish nation. In both the Old and New Testaments we have prophecies which point to the nation of Israel as a barometer of the second coming of Christ. We have seen that nation return to their homeland after centuries of dispersion, and be "born at once" (Isaiah 66:8).

4. Tribulation and the End

a. Post-Tribulation Teaching

The Post-Tribulation teaching is that the Church will go through the Great Tribulation and will be delivered after having overcome the dangers of the mark of the Beast and the tribulation. According to this teaching, the testing of the Great Tribulation will confirm the faith of the saints and they will come out of that test victoriously. This view interprets the souls under the altar (Revelation 6:9) and the saints who come through "great tribulation" as representing the entire Church of all ages. There are problems with this view, not the least of which is that it essentially sets a time for the Lord's coming.

b. The Mid-Tribulation Teaching

A teaching which seeks a balance between the "Post" and the "Pre" Tribulation teachings is that of a Mid-Tribulation return of Christ. This view generally accepts that the first half of the Great Tribulation will be a time of deception by the Antichrist and that it will not represent the awful time of wrath poured out on the world. There are several indications that the seven years are divided (Daniel 7:25; Revelation 11:2 and 13:5). This view holds that the saints might well live through the first half of the Great Tribulation without knowing that the Antichrist is in place and that the rapture of the Church will bring about the conditions which will lead to the great outpouring of God's judgmental wrath.

c. Pre-Tribulation Teaching

The Pre-Tribulation teaching concerning the return of Christ is the accepted view of the majority of Pentecostal scholars. This teaching is that Christ will come before the Great Tribulation begins and the man of sin is revealed. There are several things which commend this teaching to those who believe in the imminent return of Christ — that He could come at any time. First, the events of the Great Tribulation in Scripture are so precise and detailed that it would be difficult to mistake them. If these are to happen before the rapture, then it would be difficult to see how the rapture could happen at any time or what our Lord meant by saying that it would catch many people by surprise. One point of confusion is that the Bible does teach that saints will go through tribulation. Is this the "Great Tribulation?"

Tribulation has been present from the earliest days of the Christian Church. Yet this tribulation is not the "Great Tribulation" promised by the Word of God. The Great Tribulation is clearly judgmental. It is God's wrath poured out on sinful men. In Paul's teaching to the Thessalonian church, he told about the coming "sudden destruction" of God's wrath. He told them, "For God hath not appointed us to wrath, but to obtain salvation by our Lord Jesus Christ" (1 Thessalonians 5:9). The Psalmist tells us, "Only with thine eyes shalt thou behold and see the reward of the wicked" (Psalm 91:8).

B. His Return is Personal

1. It is Actual

In the light of the scriptures, there can be no reasonable doubt that the return of Christ is an actual return of His person and not some type of allegory or symbolism. The Bible clearly shows that the Apostles expected the Lord to return bodily and that He would be just as much the same Jesus as He was following the resurrection. In every age, there have been believers eagerly expecting the Lord to come and they always interpreted this as a physical return "in like manner" as He went away.

2. It is Visible

The message given by the angels when Christ ascended was that He would come "in like manner" or in visible form. They had seen Him go away in person. He went into physical clouds. He told His followers He would come again. He will be seen by every eye (Revelation 1:7).

3. It is Glorious

The body of our Lord is called glorious (Philippians 3:21) and His appearing for His church is called glorious: "Looking for that blessed hope, and the glorious appearing of the great God and our Saviour Jesus Christ" (Titus 2:13).

C. Rapture of the Saints

1. Bodily Resurrection

The word "rapture" is not used in the Bible, but it is commonly used today to define what happens as described in 1 Thessalonians 4:16,17: "For the Lord himself shall descend from heaven with a shout, with the voice of the archangel, and with the trump of God: and the dead in Christ shall rise first: then we which are alive and remain shall be caught up together with them in the clouds, to meet the Lord in the air: and so shall we ever be with the Lord."

a. Nature of the Resurrection

In Paul's first letter to the church at Corinth, he dealt extensively with the subject of the resurrection in the fifteenth chapter. In Philippians 3:21, Paul tells us that our resurrection bodies will be like Christ's own glorious body. The resurrection body will be incapable of pain or of death. It will be an immortal, incorruptible body. Its glory will be far above that of our present bodies. The human body is one of the most amazing elements in all of creation. Science is continually amazed at the complexity, the wonder and the perfection of the human body. Yet this body is subject to deformity, to pain and suffering and finally, to death. These limitations and imperfections will all be replaced with a perfect body which will endure for all the ages of eternity.

b. Immortal Bodies

"This mortality must put on immortality" said Paul. Our bodies are limited by time and space. Our immortal bodies will know no such limitations. As Jesus could walk through closed doors after His resurrection, so will our new bodies be unlimited in their conquest of matter. Jesus taught that all of our relationships in eternity will be real, but different than those we know now. No wonder eye has not seen and ear not heard the glories which God has prepared for His children.

"In a moment, in the twinkling of an eye, at the last trump: for the trumpet shall sound, and the dead shall be raised incorruptible, and we shall be changed" (1 Corinthians 15:52). This is what Paul calls the glorious hope of the church. It is that which undergirds our faith and brings an eternal dimension to our hopes. Because He lives, we too shall live and shall share the glories of His resurrection life.

2. The First Resurrection

The rapture of the saints is called the "first resurrection." In Revelation 20:6, we read, "Blessed and holy is he that hath part in the first resurrection: on such the second death hath no power, but they shall be priests of God and of Christ, and shall reign with him a thousand years."

D. Marriage Supper of the Lamb

In the 19th chapter of Revelation, we read of the marriage supper of the Lamb — a feast prepared for the Church at the point of final union with Christ at the rapture. The placement late in the book has been a source of misunderstanding for some. The book of Revelation should not be viewed as being chronological in order. The events are not necessarily shown in the sequence in which they happen. It is generally thought that the Marriage Supper of the Lamb will take place immediately after the rapture of the Church. At the last supper, the Lord said that He would not take of that communion cup "until that day when I drink it new with you in my Father's kingdom" (Matthew 26:29).

IV. Christ's Return to Earth

A. The Great Tribulation

When the Church is raptured, there will come a time of tribulation such as the world has never seen before (Matthew 24:21). The Church has known times of tribulation and some of that tribulation has indeed been great, but what our Lord is speaking of here and what is portrayed in the book of Revelation is a tribulation unlike any from the beginning of time. It will be so great that there must be a shortening of the days lest all mankind be destroyed. Some of the details of that time of wrath are given in the book of Revelation.

B. The Man of Sin

The book of Revelation shows that there will be an evil man, the Antichrist, who will have great power in the last days. There is also a "dragon" who has great power, and another beast, forming an unholy trinity. Some have taught that the Antichrist is a system, but it seems clear from the Bible that this is to be a man. We are given some details regarding his person and his rise to power. He will come in the spirit of the "antichrists" who have long been in the world but will be of a different order. He will appear to offer great hope of peace to the world, and will make a covenant with the Jews, which he will break. This "man of sin" will help to re-establish a great world empire and will use miracles as a means of proving his power. He will war against all who differ with him and will persecute those who attempt to turn to Christ and will kill them. He will establish a mark without which people cannot engage in commerce.

There has long been speculation regarding the Antichrist. There have been many popular candidates, but the real Antichrist will be revealed when the Church is gone and the "restrainer" (2 Thessalonians 2:7) is removed. This verse indicates that the Antichrist will not be revealed until after the rapture of the Church.

C. The Battle of Armageddon

In the 16th chapter of Revelation, we find the description of the final great battle placed at Megiddo or "Armageddon." Daniel 11 also gives us some details of this final battle. The nations of the world will be arrayed against each other on two sides, but when Jesus appears riding on a white horse, and followed by His saints, the antagonists will turn and fight against Him. However, He will quickly bring the battle to an end in what will be the most bloody of all battles, and will exercise His authority over not only earthly powers but over Satan as well.

D. Consummation of the Age

The dispensational approach to history makes our time the Church age or the "age of the Gentiles." This age will end with the overthrow of the

Antichrist and of Satan and the world will be prepared for a new epoch. And just as all of nature changed when Adam and Eve sinned, so will all of nature change with the coming of the "Second Adam" of Jesus Christ. Since the end of the dispensation of innocence, no age has demonstrated such radical change as will come when Christ sets up His kingdom of peace here on earth.

E. Christ's Reign on Earth

Revelation 20:6 makes clear that the final dispensation before eternity will last for one thousand years. It is from this that we get the name "Millennium," which is Latin for "thousand years." Let us explore some of the theories which exist regarding the reign of Christ on earth.

1. Postmillennialism

Postmillennialists teach that the thousand years will end before the coming of Christ. According to this teaching, the Church will exert its influence in the world until it becomes a righteous world and the leaven of the Gospel alters all which is evil. They do not suppose that this will mean that all men will become Christian or that all evil is eradicated, but that the world will gradually become a better and better place until it is ready for the Lord to come and take up His reign of righteousness.

2. Amillennialism

Those holding the amillennial position feel that there will not be a true "thousand year" reign of Christ, but rather that the Church will prepare the world for the coming of Christ and that all of the dead will be resurrected at the same time and the Great Judgment will take place immediately. This view generally holds that Christ bound Satan after

Calvary, and that we are now in the period where Christ reigns through the Church.

3. Premillennialism

Pentecostals hold to the premillennial position — the truth that Jesus will come for His saints and that the "dead in Christ" will rise to be with the Lord in the air. We hold that Jesus will establish a true thousand-year reign on earth following His glorious triumph at Armageddon. We believe that there will be a great "falling away" as we near the coming of the Lord, and that the millennial reign of our Lord will end with the Great White Throne Judgment and the beginning of eternity.

V. Errors and Alternative Beliefs

A. Jehovah's Witnesses

Jehovah's Witnesses, following the teaching of their founder, Charles Russell, believe that Jesus came secretly and invisibly in 1914 and that He came to "the spiritual temple" in 1918. According to their doctrine, the Jehovah's Witnesses are God's sole witnesses who are charged with the task of preparing the world for the new kingdom of Christ.

B. Seventh Day Adventists

Seventh Day Adventism grew out of a dangerous mistake: setting a day for the Lord's return. A sincere Christian by the name of William Miller decided that Daniel's prophecy (Daniel 8:14) showed that Christ would return in 1843. When this did not happen, one of his followers declared that an error in computation had been made. The date would be precisely September 22, 1844. Another of the followers decided that Christ had come to "cleanse the heavenly sanctuary," and thus did Ellen G. White proclaim in the founding of the Adventist organization. Thus, they believe that Christ has already come and that worshipping on Sunday constitutes the "mark of the beast."

C. Spiritism

Spiritism teaches that the souls of all people who die survive in spheres near the earth and that these souls can be reached through their seances. They do not believe in any of the Christian doctrines related to the end of time and judgment. In earlier years, the spiritists denounced Christianity, but now they often seek to influence and infiltrate those churches which have no sure faith in God's Word.

D. Liberal Theology

Modernism in its many forms adopts the popular psychology which states that sins are the result of normal human urges which are not basically evil and are often the results of environment and heredity. They believe that guilt is not justified; therefore they renounce any belief in human accountability in eternity or any judgment to come. For many, there is little faith that there will be life after death.

Questions for Review

1. What happens when a believer dies?
2. Where does the sinner go at death?
3. Where does the idea of Purgatory come from?
4. How do we know that Jesus will return physically?
5. Why is it dangerous to set a time for Christ's return?
6. What is the great danger of "Post-tribulation" teaching?
7. Is the word "Rapture" in the Bible?
8. How does the "Great Tribulation" differ from other tribulation?
9. What battle will bring the Millennial kingdom of Christ into being?
10. What error do the Jehovah's Witnesses and Seventh Day Adventists share?

13

JUDGMENT

Outline

I. Christ's Reign on Earth
A. Satan Bound
B. Earthly Inhabitants
C. Role of the Saints
D. Temple Restored
E. Peaceful Kingdom
   1. Curse Lifted
   2. Peace Restored
   3. Life Extended

II. Satan's Final Effort
A. Loosed for a Season
B. Testing of All Citizens
C. Christ Accepted or Rejected

III. Judgments
A. Christ's Bema Judgment
B. Judgment of the Nations
C. Great White Throne Judgment
D. Satan's Destiny

IV. Eternity
    A. For the Saints
       1. New Heavens and Earth
    B. For the Lost
       1. It is Forever
       2. Is Damnation Unjust?
V. Errors and Alternative Beliefs
    A. Universalism
    B. Temporary Punishment

I. Christ's Reign on Earth

It can be rightly said that judgment happens at the coming of Christ, for all the righteous living and dead will go to be with Him in the clouds of glory. While this is not specifically called a judgment in the Bible, it has the effect of judging all living and dead humanity. It also establishes the thousand-year reign of Christ after His victory over the Antichrist and his followers at Armageddon.

A. Satan Bound

The reign of Christ on earth begins with the binding of Satan for the thousand-year period (Revelation 20:2). The deceptions which have caused so many to refuse Christ will end for the duration of this righteous reign. From his fall, Satan has enjoyed great liberty among creation to practice his deception and lying. This deception will be totally out of harmony with the righteousness of Christ's reign, so the tempter will be removed until that reign is completed.

B. Earthly Inhabitants

It is clear that there will be mortals living following the great final battle and that it will be over these that our Lord will reign. They will include many Jews who accept Christ after the rapture of the Church. In Isaiah 11, we see some details of this time. The ninth verse tells us that the earth will be full of the knowledge of the Lord "as the waters cover the sea."

C. Role of the Saints

Revelation 1:5 and 5:10 tell us that the saints will reign with Christ as kings and priests. Paul told Timothy: "If we suffer, we shall also reign with him" (2 Timothy 2:12). We are not told the full extent to which these duties will apply, but it would seem evident that Christ will draw His civil and spiritual rulers from the ransomed saints who return with Him to set up His righteous reign on earth.

D. Temple Restored

Jerusalem will once again be the true spiritual headquarters of earth and a new Temple will be there and will become the focus of all worship as Christ establishes His presence there. The Moslems keep the eastern gate to the ancient walls of Jerusalem sealed for fear that Jesus will come in through it and establish His reign. They will be powerless to stop Him when the time comes, for He will reign there and the Temple will be restored.

E. Peaceful Kingdom

As noted, Isaiah 11 gives significant details regarding the kingdom of Christ during the Millennium. From these, we can see that there will be great changes in the world in which our Lord will reign.

1. Curse Lifted

The Bible consistently identifies Christ with Adam and He is called the "second Adam." The first Adam sinned and because of his sin, a curse fell on the earth. That curse included sickness and physical death and it also brought thorns and thistles, and savagery among the beasts. Through Christ, the "Second Adam," this will be reversed and the animals will once again enjoy a life without fear. Wolves will dwell peacefully with lambs. Bears and cows will feed together. The curse brought by sin will in large part be removed in that wonderful day.

   2. Peace Restored

In Micah 4:3, we see that there will be no need for swords. In our day, nations spend tremendous portions of their wealth on armaments. There will be no need of this waste in that day, for there will be no rivalry among nations and no danger to households. The peace for which the world has so long yearned will at last become a reality. The Prince of Peace will bring peace to this world.

   3. Life Extended

Isaiah once again gives us information regarding the nature of life during the Millennium. Life will be lengthened and death will not be so common as it is now (Isaiah 65:20-23). Life will be much closer to that of Eden than to life in our own day. The reign of Christ will bring to men the longings of their hearts and will show that righteousness and equity bring happiness and true pleasure.

II. Satan's Final Effort

   A. Loosed for a Season

In Revelation 20:7, we see that Satan will be released from his bondage for a short period of time at the end of the Millennium. Why would God allow this to happen? We must remember that the Lord will not make anybody go to Heaven. All who inherit eternal life must do so by willingly accepting Christ and making Him Lord of their lives. The perfection of their society and their world does not mean that there will not be room for temptation and for other desires. Satan will always be the deceiver.

B. Testing of All Citizens

Adam and Eve had it all. They had a perfect world with a perfect relationship with God. Yet there was room in their hearts for coveting, and for unholy aspirations. The mortals living during the Millennium will also have a world so much more perfect and harmonious than our own that it is difficult to see how they could be tempted to reject Christ. Yet Satan is skilled as a deceiver. He knows how to promise what he cannot deliver. All who inherit an eternity with God will do so through accepting Christ and by overcoming testing. The binding of Satan will enable Christ to set up His kingdom of peace, but the necessity of choice will make it necessary to subject those mortals to the rigors of satanic testing and temptation. Only thus may they truly choose to serve the Lord and to be worthy of God's eternal blessings.

C. Christ Accepted or Rejected

When Satan is loosed for that season of time, all mortals will find it necessary to make a choice. Like Pilate and the Jews, they must determine what they will do with Jesus. We can only imagine the methods Satan will contrive during the thousand years and the temptations which he will place before the mortals in the world. They must decide and that choice will seal their eternal destinies.

III. Judgments

There are a variety of interpretations as to just what judgments are taught in the Bible. Some appear to be given different names in different locations, but there are some which are commonly accepted as being distinct and separate. Of course, there are judgments past. The cross was truly a judgment of God and Christ broke the power of Satan at Calvary. It is also true that the rapture of the Church constitutes a judgment, inasmuch as the righteous are raptured thus determining who are Christ's at that time. However, the three judgments included here are future events which are spoken of as judgments in the Word of God.

A. Christ's Bema Judgment

In 2 Corinthians 5:10 we read: "For we must all appear before the judgment seat of Christ; that every one may receive the things done in his body, according to that he hath done, whether it be good or bad." When we look at 1 Corinthians 3, we find that the works of the believer will be judged. The word used by Paul is "bema," which is taken from the Olympic games in which the ruler would sit on a throne and give out rewards to the victors. Paul is speaking to the Christians and he is confirming that Christ will give rewards according to our faithfulness. This is further supported by Christ's teachings regarding faithful stewardship. This is not a judgment separating the righteous from the unrighteous but one in which the believers are rewarded "according to the deeds." What a revelation that judgment will be for those who thought all the Christian life meant was getting to Heaven!

B. Judgment of the Nations

In Matthew 25:31-46, our Lord details a judgment of nations. Some have interpreted this to be another description of the final Great White Throne Judgment, but there are differences which we must consider. It would appear that this judgment is a literal judgment of nations according to their treatment of the Jews. God does not save nations in the spiritual sense of the word. This judgment appears to take place at the beginning of the Millennium and thus, to determine the relationship and blessings nations are to receive during Christ's reign. We must never lose sight of the special relationship which God has established with the Jews and the enduring consequences of that relationship. Until the final words of prophecy, God's Word declares a special consideration to be given to these chosen people and a special call to them to accept Christ.

C. Great White Throne Judgment

In the 20th chapter of Revelation, we see a description of the final judgment: The Great White Throne Judgment. This is the place where time is separated from eternity. It is here that all the lost will come for final judgment. While it is possible that the raptured saints will be spectators of that awful event (see Psalm 91:8), they will not face any judgment themselves. Those who have lived on earth as mortals during the Millennium would appear to be the only redeemed people judged at that event.

D. Satan's Destiny

In this judgment, we will also see the final judgment on Satan and his angels. Satan will try to war against Christ, but fire will come down from God and all who follow Satan will be cast into the lake of fire and brimstone (sulphur). Then all the dead will stand before God and the books are opened. It is from the books of God that men will be judged. Jesus told that some would stand there and tell of miracles they had done, but would be rejected because they are not known to God. Everyone whose name is not written in the book of life will be cast into the lake of fire with Satan and his followers. This is called the second death.

IV. Eternity

A. For the Saints

1. New heavens and New Earth

Revelation 21 tells us that God will make a new heaven and a new earth for the beginning of eternity. There will then be a new Jerusalem which will come down from God out of heaven and will house the tabernacle of God in that new, eternal city. It is here that we will see the splendors promised. It will be a city so great that gold will be as common as asphalt in our day and will pave the streets. The precious stones for which men fight and die will be so common that they will make up the walls of the city. All that is beautiful and all that is precious will be there in great abundance.

We also find that the perfect splendors of Eden will be restored to men there. The tree of life will be there and the river. Jesus will be the light of that land and there will be no night. No wonder Paul said that "eye hath not seen, nor ear heard, neither have entered into the heart of man, the things which God hath prepared for them that love him" (1 Corinthians 2:9).

B. For the Lost

" . . . the fearful, and the unbelieving, and the abominable, and murderers, and whoremongers, and sorcerers, and idolators, and all liars, shall have their part in the lake which burneth with fire and brimstone: which is the second death" (Revelation 21:8). This is one of the most thought-provoking verses in the Bible, for it portrays so vividly the destiny of all who reject Christ and who live and die in their sins.

1. It is Forever

Revelation 10:10 makes abundantly clear that the punishment of the wicked is forever. There is absolutely no implication that there will ever be an end of the pain and isolation of the lake of fire. Some have tried to build theories from Scripture to support the idea of limited punishment. In Matthew 25:41 and 46, Jesus called it "everlasting punishment." In the ninth chapter of Mark, we find words of Jesus which speak of the lake of fire as where "the worm dieth not and the fire is not quenched." The "worm" clearly speaks of the soul. We should also understand that when the "eternal" is used in Scripture, the same word is used for eternal punishment as is used for eternal life or eternal blessedness.

2. Is Damnation Unjust?

Critics have contended that the Christian teaching of eternal punishment is inconsistent with the love of God. Sinful men are drawn to the teaching of God's love and mercy, but to take those teachings and not the clear lessons of the Word regarding punishment is to humanize the book. Certainly God is a God of mercy and of great love, but He is also a God who is holy and who cannot dwell where unholiness exists. It was not arrogance when our Lord said that He is the Way, the Truth and the Life. It is simple fact. Anything less than the truth will lead men to a false sense of well-being and of carelessness.

God loves men so much that He gave His only begotten Son to redeem all who will come in His name. The way of salvation is available to all men and God made a plan of salvation which any man can find and follow. When man refuses to accept God's offer of eternal life and refuses to accept Christ as Lord, he rebels against God and is therefore united with Satan in the conspiracy against God. There can be only one just and one perfect solution to that rebellion and it is to be united with Satan in eternal damnation. Just as God will make no man go to Heaven against his will, He will also send no man to hell against his will, for it is the will of man which determines his final destiny. John 3:16 makes this abundantly clear.

V. Errors and Alternative Beliefs

A. Universalism

There is a broad teaching shared by many cults and some liberal Christian people which contends that God is the Father of all and that God will ultimately take all people to Heaven with Him. This teaching most often includes all religions in universal redemption and they major on the "Fatherhood of God and the brotherhood of man." The New Age movement is a prominent proponent of this idea. This teaching is totally at odds with the plain teachings of our Lord. He taught that there is only one door to Heaven and that is through our Lord. Universalism sounds benevolent and it has great appeal to men, but the Bible clearly teaches that there is a path to eternal life and the way to God is narrow and straight. This is not narrow-mindedness; it is simply truth.

B. Temporary Punishment

Another false teaching related to judgment is that all evil men will be annihilated at the judgment. They believe the souls of the dead sleep until the day of judgment, then all the wicked will be destroyed. The adventists do believe that there will be a brief time of conscious torment for the lost, but the Jehovah's Witnesses believe that the lost cease to exist at death.

Questions for Review

1. What elements of Eden will be restored in Christ's reign?
2. What will the saints be doing during the Millennium?
3. What will happen to Satan during the Millennium?
4. Why is Satan to be loosed at the end of Christ's reign?
5. Will any mortals living during the Millennium be lost?
6. What is the "Bema" Judgment?
7. What is the purpose of the Great White Throne Judgment?
8. What is Satan's ultimate destiny?
9. When does the New Jerusalem appear?
10. Why is no sun needed in eternity?